Old Order Mennonites

Old Order Mennonites

Rituals, Beliefs, and Community

Daniel B. Lee
The Pennsylvania State University

Burnham Inc., Publishers

Chicago

President: Kathleen Kusta
Vice-President: Brett J. Hallongren
General Manager: Richard O. Meade
Project Editor: Rachel Schick
Designer: Tamra Phelps
Typesetter: Camron Publishing Services
Printer: Cushing-Malloy, Inc.
Cover Art: "Rural Route" by Gil Beamsley

Most of the photographs in this book were taken by the author and illustrate real farms and landscapes of Old Order Mennonite life.

Library of Congress Cataloging-in-Publication Data

Lee, Daniel B.
    Old Order Mennonites : rituals, beliefs, and community / Daniel B. Lee.
        p. cm.
    Includes bibliographical references.
    ISBN 0-8304-1573-4 (paper : alk. paper)
    1. Old Order Mennonite Church. Weaverland Conference. 2. New York
    (State)—Religious life and customs. 3. Old Order Mennonites—New
York (State) 1. Title.

    BX8129.O43 L44 2000
    289.71'747—dc21

                                                                00-033739

Manufactured in the United States of America

10 9 8 7 6 5 4 3 2 1

∞ The paper used in this book meets the minimum requirements of American National Standard for Information Sciences—Permanence of Paper for Printed Library Materials, ANSI Z39.48-1984.

Contents

Foreword

This is a sociological study of the rituals and beliefs of a religious community, the Weaverland Conference of Old Order Mennonites. It is an ethnography, resulting from almost three years of observation and participation.

I think the life-style of Old Order Mennonites is intriguing and quickly captures the interest of outsiders. Understanding the history, traditions, and social institutions of this Mennonite community helps one appreciate the richness of American culture. Contemporary "Plain People" continue to resist assimilation with mainstream society, despite the fact that their ancestors were among the first colonial pioneers.

This book illustrates the religious life of a special community, but it also suggests a general theory of ritual, belief, and social solidarity. I suggest that shared religious beliefs and ideas do not appear to integrate members of the Mennonite community. Rather, Mennonites are united by their behavior in everyday life—by their common practices, rituals, and conformity to rules. When members of a social group act according to the same rules, society becomes possible. With this study, I explain how social rituals are enacted on the basis of rules, not shared beliefs. Beliefs remain hidden in the minds of members. An individual's own religious convictions may be of great personal value, but they do not equip one to be social.

Religious beliefs and ideas are *inside* people, but rituals are *between* them.

This book could not have been written without the kind assistance and openness of Weaverland Mennonites. I am especially indebted to George V. Zito for many years of professional guidance and mentoring. William McCarthy generously gave of his renowned proofreading ability.

My undergraduate research assistants, Tami Principe and Jamie Thrush, contributed valuable insights. At Burnham, Richard Meade, my editor, and this book's designer, Tamra Phelps, made the final production of this volume an author's delight.

I am most thankful for the friendly support and critical advice of my wife, Eva Lee.

Chapter 1

Introduction: "A Different People"

Religion should our thoughts engage
  Amidst our youthful bloom;
'Twill fit us for declining age,
  And for the awful gloom.[1]

If my neighbor's cow had not gone dry, I may never have visited the Mennonite family down the road. I was told that the family operates a dairy and sells fresh milk to some of their neighbors. I went to the farm and bought two quarts, an action that resulted in my writing this book.

It was immediately apparent that the members of the family were different from most rural Americans. I stopped by in the evening, during milking time, accompanied by my neighbor Mrs. Clayton, who insisted that she ought to come along and make introductions. We found the whole family in the barn. Five young children were each hard at work at their own chores: cleaning udders, scooping manure, and distributing feed. Their youngest brother, about three years old, was fast asleep on top of some empty feed bags. The three girls wore their long hair in braids. The boys all had short hair, slickly parted on the same side. A woman appeared from around a row of black and white cows pushing a heavily loaded wheelbarrow of feed. Despite her small frame, the well-formed muscles in her arms were impressive. She wore a dress, extending below her knees, and a white covering on her head. When she greeted us, I could clearly detect a "Pennsylvania Dutch" accent. "Hello, would you be here for milk? My husband will be right along. Go fetch your father, Mary Ellen."

When the farmer appeared, I explained that I lived a few miles down the road, next to Mrs. Clayton, and would like to start buying milk. He said, "Uh huh. You want to buy milk. I see. Mrs. Clayton told you that you could get milk here?" His wife and children had interrupted their work and stood around observing the interaction. "Well," I replied, "My neighbor, Mrs. Clayton, mentioned that you might sell me some, since her cow went dry." Mrs. Clayton, who never loses words, silently nodded with a smile. "Uh huh," the dairyman said, "we do sometimes sell milk, but not openly. State don't allow it, on account of health problems. It's good enough for us though. If you want some, you can come by at this time any day, except on Sundays. This is when we do the evening milking."

As we drove away from the dairy, my neighbor whispered, "Those are different people, they're Mennonites." I did not tell Mrs. Clayton that I was happy about her cow having gone dry. As a sociologist and curious person, this special family had captured my complete attention. I wanted to learn more about this family, their way of life, and the religion that made them "different people." I returned for more milk, again and again.

After buying those first two quarts of milk, I became much better acquainted with the members of the family. We worked and played together during the next several years. I came to know their relatives and friends. I started regularly attending their worship services and congregational events.

By observing and participating in the social life of the Mennonite community, I have learned some of the reasons why they really *are* different from most Americans. The members of this community refer to themselves as the Weaverland Conference of Old Order Mennonites. They consciously strive to be a "peculiar people," separate from "the world."[2]

Valuing strict conformity to traditional religious practices, members of this community appear, at first glance, to lack individuality. Among the characteristics that they share, members are typically farmers, attend the same church, wear the same old-fashioned clothing, and drive the same unusual "black-bumpered" vehicles. After becoming more familiar with members of the church, however, I have found that beneath the uniform surface a great deal of diversity actually exists. In this study, I suggest that an unacknowledged dualism appears to exist at the heart of this Mennonite community: this society seems characterized by uniformity in action, yet diversity in thought.

The members of this religious community perform the same actions, but give different reasons for their actions. This phenomenon is well illustrated by the following example. One of the most important rituals practiced by Mennonites is exchanging the "kiss of peace" after observing Communion and Foot Washing. The *Con-*

fession of Faith of the Mennonite (*COF*), a little black book given
to all members at the time of baptism, precisely describes how the
kiss ought to be performed:

> Then both shake hands with each other and give each
> other the kiss of peace, whereupon the one says: "The
> Lord will preserve and strengthen us in love;" the other
> says "Amen." (*COF* 1996: 56)

After watching Mennonites perform this ritual for the first
time, I was curious to know what they were whispering to each
other. I had not yet discovered the existence of the *COF*. After
church I asked an older man what was said after the kiss. He said,
"We always say the same thing: one of us gives a greeting and the
other says 'amen.' The words of the greeting are important, they
are: 'May the Lord guard, guide, and direct you.'" I inquired how
the two decide who will give the greeting and who will say "amen."
"That's easy," the man replied, "the one who had his feet washed
first says the amen."

I walked over to another member and inquired about the
words exchanged. Once again, it was claimed that "everyone says
the same thing, a greeting and an amen." However, this time the
words of the greeting were different: "May the Lord love and protect you."

"Amen."

After I interviewed a third member of the church about the
words used in the greeting, the reason for the different responses
became clearer:

> AUTHOR: After members exchanged the "kiss of peace," I saw
> them lean over and whisper into each other's ears. Can you
> tell me what was said?
> MEMBER: Well, one says the greeting and the other says
> "amen."

A: What kind of greeting is it? Does everybody say the same thing?

M: Everyone says the same thing.

A: Can you tell me what words are used?

M: Yes. . . We say, "May the Lord. . . (mumbles something)." Like that, then the other says "Amen."

A: I'm sorry, I didn't hear the words of the greeting. What are they again?

M: You just have to say "May the Lord. . . (mumbles)," you know. Then the other says "Amen."

A: But, David, what are the exact words used in the greeting?

M: I'll tell you the truth (smiling). We are supposed to say the same thing, but I don't really know the exact words. I just say "May the Lord. . . " and mumble something. I know most of the guys don't really know what to say. They never told us exactly what to say. The important thing is to make it look right.

Since members are supposed to study their personal copy of the *COF*, they should all know the exact wording of the "correct" greeting. Yet they do not know. The important thing, it seems, is to "make it look right." When asked about the religious significance of the "kiss of peace," members of the church were almost always prepared to give an explanation, but an explanation tainted with idiosyncrasy:

- Our ancestors brought the kiss with them from Germany and Switzerland. We want to hold on to those traditions.
- The kiss was established by the early leaders of the church. Mennonites just believe in doing it.
- It's from the Bible. The disciples did it.
- It's something we have always done.
- I don't know why we do it.

Mennonites and other "Plain People" will actually conform to the behavioral rules of their church even if they have strong personal reservations against them. Returning to the practice of the "kiss of peace," the following letter to the editor of an Old Order periodical is illuminating. The letter was published in *Family Life*, a journal widely read among the Mennonites I became familiar with. The author of the letter complains about having to give the kiss to his brethren and confesses that he attaches no spiritual significance to the kiss:

> Holy kissing makes many miserable. It's so repulsive! That spit spot on the lips and that irresistible urge to wipe off one's mouth with the back of your hand first chance he's not looking, is anything but a feeling of holiness. It's so germy and unsanitary. Glasses often clack together. Often on cold days it's not just spit on the lips but catarrh or nose drip on the cheek. I'm not trying to be sarcastic! (*Family Life* 1984a: 3)

The author concludes his letter by arguing that the church should do away with the holy kiss as traditionally practiced. However, until this happens, we may be certain that he and his spiritual brothers will continue to exchange the kiss of peace whether or not they "believe" in the custom.

In another letter to the same Old Order periodical, a Plain woman wrote about her emotional desire to greet a friend with the kiss. Unfortunately (from the woman's point of view), because the rules of the church regulate precisely to whom the greeting may be given, the kiss could not be bestowed.

> When I think of the holy kiss, there is always a memory that haunts me. Of an old lady in a hospital bed, whom I was too righteous to kiss. . . . known her since I was a little girl, since she'd sold my parents the farm we grew up on. She'd been like a Grandma to us. . . .

But now I was visiting her in a hospital where she'd been a patient for two weeks. She was weak and her skin had a strange color. . . .

I thought of this lady living alone for years already, no family, now in a far-away hospital, starving for affection. I knew what I should do, but I thought, "I can't kiss you—you don't belong to our church." (*Family Life* 1984a: 3)

In this encounter, the author of the letter laments that she is not allowed to extend spiritual greetings to people who are not members of her church. On a rational level, she knows that she cannot give the kiss to anyone except a spiritual sister, even if she believes that she ought to give it to her sick friend. She conforms to a rule of her community even though she believes that the rule reflects a hypocritical and self-righteous attitude.

One final letter to the editor of *Family Life* is worth noting. Here, an Old Order man strongly defends the holy kiss, but he does so without ever suggesting that he believes that the practice, in itself, has any kind of spiritual or personal significance. Rather, he claims that members need to continue the practice because, quite simply, that is what they have always done:

The 1568 Conference (Diener Versammlung) has among 20 articles that brethren and sisters, each to each, greet each other with the kiss of the Lord. These articles were again confirmed and other articles added in the conferences of 1607, 1630, 1668, 1752, 1755. Again in Germany a conference drew up 16 articles. At least 22 Amish districts were represented with 48 ministers present. Article 10: Each brother or sister shall greet each other brother or sister with the kiss of the Lord.

God is a God of order and His word gives the correct order. (*Family Life* 1984a: 3)

Members of the Weaverland Mennonite church mutually value an outward demonstration of social order and coordinated unity, but understand the meaning of their collective behavior in different ways. This diversity on the level of meaning, this *hetero-doxis*, is hidden behind striking *orthopraxis*, conformity to the rules of ritual participation and mass adherence to the strict behavioral regulations of the church.

A Problem of
Social Integration

The uniformity-diversity dualism at the root of this Mennonite society poses a fascinating sociological problem. *Is there necessarily a commonly held meaning behind collective action?* The individual members of the community discussed in this book demonstrate remarkably high conformity in their behavior. However, these Old Order Mennonites provide very different accounts and justifications for participating in their religious rituals and abiding by the church regulations. With this in mind, to what extent do members share a common understanding of their behavior?

The uniformity observed in Mennonite action belies the diversity of what members think. When asked to explain the religious significance of washing feet or the Holy Communion, individuals give different accounts. This makes sense, as the community does not make an attempt to cultivate leaders with specialized religious knowledge, monitor the "correctness" of each member's beliefs, or provide members with systematic religious education.

This Old Order Mennonite community does not have a formal means by which members are effectively taught "official" religious beliefs. The group does not conduct Sunday School, train its spiritual leaders, or formally educate children past the age of 14. Ministers are selected from the congregation by lot and are expected to continue in their secular occupations. Hence, individual members tend to come to their own conclusions about the "real meaning" of religious rituals and regulations. As a consequence, their actions are explained in different voices, revealing heterodoxis.

This diversity of belief, however, does not appear to threaten the integration of group members or their ability to coordinate collective interaction. The membership evidently glosses over its lack of orthodoxis, acting *as if* there was intersubjective agreement as to the official and correct interpretation of their religious action. In the words of the early American sociologist W.I. Thomas, "social situations defined as real are real in their consequences." Mennonites define their social situation as uniform, and *take for granted* that they all hold the same beliefs—creating the real consequence of increased social integration.

In this book, I raise questions about the relationship between social thought and social action. As a sociologist, I have been trained to seek an understanding of the intentions of social actors. Why do people do the things they do? Why do members of a community perform the same actions? I have been taught to assume that thought precedes action, and that religious action, such as ritual, expresses previously formed religious ideas. In order to understand the actions of a church, the sociologist simply asks members about their religious beliefs. But can a group of individuals participate in the activity of a religious community without sharing the same beliefs? How similar must the personal beliefs of group members be? If beliefs are not the same for all members, how are religious practices such as ritual coordinated? *If the members of a social group are not united in their thoughts, how can they be united in their actions?*

My observations of Old Order Mennonites in New York State convince me to reject a commonly accepted assumption among students of religion; namely, that collective beliefs necessarily play an essential role in social life. In my view, common practices pervade the whole social life of Mennonites while common beliefs are nowhere to be found. Mennonites, as well as members of other religious communities, take for granted that they share religious beliefs with their peers—even though these beliefs do not exist. In this book, I demonstrate that this disjuncture on the level of belief does not disrupt the harmony of life in the community.

Methods of Data Collection

To collect information about this community, I used qualitative research methods commonly used by sociologists when "working in the field." I presented myself to members of the group as a "sociologist" and asked if I could learn about their community. I remained in the field for two and a half years; gathering data by interviewing members, reading Old Order Mennonite magazines and literature, studying church membership records and historical documents, and directly observing and participating in community events.

I tried to be present at as many different community events as possible, always making my best effort to become involved in the life of the group. I regularly went to church, to singings, and to special congregational events. I spent time at the cattle auction with the men and watched women practice the art of quilting. I helped make egg noodles, pull weeds, pick strawberries, butcher cows, repair tractors, and construct buildings. My relationship to this Weaverland community may best be described as "participant-observer." As a social scientist, however, I remained an outsider. "Qualitative ethnographic social research entails an attitude of detachment toward society that permits the sociologist to observe the conduct of self and others, to understand the mechanisms of social processes, and to comprehend and explain why both actors and processes are as they are" (Vidich and Lyman 1994: 23).

My status as a nonmember was evident from the first encounter I had with members of this group. It took many months of building familiarity and trust before friendships could develop. Though there are members of the church with whom I could, in private, talk about any subject, there are a few members who never did express any interest in speaking to me. Weaverland Mennonites refer to themselves as "chosen people, the royal priesthood, the holy nation." As a nonmember of their church, I remained a sinner and at home in "the world." However, as a stranger I was in a good position to hear candid remarks about the church that members would not reveal to one another. The commonplace things that members of a group may take for granted remain of interest to the sociologist, the stranger, who sees them for the first time. The German sociologist Georg Simmel described the special vantage point of the one who occupies the role of stranger in a social group:

> [The stranger] is not radically committed to the unique
> ingredients and peculiar tendencies of the group, and
> therefore approaches them with the specific attitude of
> "objectivity." But objectivity does not involve passivity
> and detachment; it is a particular structure composed of
> distance and nearness, indifference and involvement. . . .
> [The stranger] often receives the most surprising open-
> ness—confidences which sometimes have the character
> of a confessional and which would be carefully withheld
> from a more closely related person. . . . [The stranger]
> is freer, practically and theoretically; he surveys condi-
> tions with less prejudice; his criteria for them are more
> general and more objective ideals; he is not tied down in
> his action by habit, piety, and precedent. (1950: 403–5)

Even as a stranger, certain aspects of my personality helped me become "accepted" into the congregation as a participant-observer. I believe that being a white male, as well as having a wife and children, increased my chances of building friendly relation-ships with members. I can speak German, sing hymns well, am familiar with the Bible, and was brought up in a "conservative" Christian church. I also enjoy working on farms, talking about cows, and eating fresh vegetables from the garden. I mention these things not only because they facilitated my entry into this community, but also because they influence the way I observe and discuss social phenomena.

In an effort to test the accuracy of my understanding of their community, I often consulted members of the group while preparing this book. I made copies of my field notes and drafts of some chapters available to members. The feedback that I received from Weaverland Conference members convinced me not to report some observations that might embarrass the community without adding value to my investigation. I also was persuaded to describe certain characteristics of the group in greater detail, especially features that members believe might improve the image of the church. Most importantly, by allowing members to read parts of my manuscript, some misunderstandings and errors were corrected.

The members that agreed to review parts of my manuscript seemed motivated, as one reader put it, by a "concern that the book will portray a true picture of the goals and efforts of the Weaverland Conference Mennonite Church." With the patient, diligent assistance offered by members of the church, I believe that I have come much closer to portraying a "true" picture. Nonetheless, readers should bear in mind that the picture portrayed in this book is not the work of a Mennonite. Furthermore, the fact that members provided me valuable assistance in this project does not mean that they agreed with my conclusions or approved of my efforts to publish a study about their community.

Members responded to my written reports in a variety of ways. It is clear that some individuals wished that I had never visited the church. Not wanting their church to be the subject of "the world's" attention, they seemed irritated that I decided to write about it. It is possible that they do not understand why a sociologist would want to learn about them. Others suggested that my questions and interpretations helped them better understand what they value about their community. A few individuals indicated that my observations might convince members of the need to change some aspects of their collective life. My admiration for Weaverland

Mennonites precludes any desire to alter the characteristics of their community.

Notes

1. *A Collection of Psalms and Hymns* 1977: 235.

2. Very little has been published about the Weaver and Mennonites. The group was briefly noted in the *The Mennonite Encyclopedia* (1959: 47–49, 905), Schlabach (1985), and Benowitz (1996). Descendents of Bishop Jonas H. Martin published his biography and genealology (Martin and Martin 1985). The community is described by Weaver (1989), in his book about the Weaverland Mennonites of the Lancaster Conference. In his *Introduction to Old Order and Conservative Mennonite Groups*, Scott (1996) includes a chapter that discusses the Weaverland Conference and two other groups of "automobile Mennonites."

A member of the Weaverland Church produced an exceptional collection of historical documents about Bishop Martin, the schism, and the development of the new church (Hoover 1982). Hoover, known by his brethren as "historical Amos," seems to be the primary source of information about the Weaverland Conference.

Weaverland members occasionally write about their group's history and early leaders in their monthly church newsletter, the *Home Messenger* (most notable is the "Moses Horning Memorial Issue," May 1977). For use by its members, the Weaverland Church has published a membership directory that includes an account of the history, organization, and size of the church (Wise and Martin 1990; 1995).

Chapter 2

The Origins of the Weaverland Conference Mennonites

A charge to keep I have,
A God to glorify,
A never-dying soul to save,
And fit it for the sky.[1]

It seems that the Weaverland Old Order Mennonite community began with a stolen pulpit. The mysterious theft occurred during the night of September 26, 1889. Members of the Lancaster Conference of Mennonites were preparing to dedicate a newly constructed Meeting House near Smoketown, Pennsylvania. All but the final touches had been completed on the building, and the first service was scheduled for the very next Sunday morning.

The wooden pulpit inside the Meeting House was, it should be noted, a controversial piece of furniture. Mennonites were accustomed to having their ministers preach while standing behind a normal table. The ministers would put their Bibles, songbooks, and glasses of water on the table. Some conservative members of the church associated the new elevated pulpit with pride, spiritual inequality, worldliness, and dangerous change. Despite sincere opposition, the Building Committee had made the decision to build the pulpit without the formal consensus of the congregation. Members of the committee claimed that the pulpit would serve as a more comfortable stand for their preacher, John Zimmerman, who had only one arm. Whatever the reasons for installing it, nobody ever saw the pulpit used.

The painters first reported the theft. On the morning of September 27, they arrived to finish their work inside the building and discovered that the pulpit had disappeared. Apparently, under the cover of darkness, someone had crept into the Meeting House through a small window and unlocked the door so that others could get in. They tore out the pulpit and filled in the hole with floorboards. In the place where the pulpit should have been, the criminals had placed an old-fashioned, poorly constructed preacher's table.

On Sunday morning, during the dedication of the new Lichty Meeting House, sermons were given in both German and English. Bishop Jonas H. Martin pronounced the benediction at the close of the service. The ministers did not even mention the missing pulpit. The stolen piece of furniture, however, was certainly what everyone was thinking about. It would take 19 years before a woman would confess that her family was responsible for the deed. (Martin and Martin 1985: 43–44; Weiler 1995: 24)

The pulpit incident immediately disrupted the peace of the church and polarized members into conservative and progressive factions. According to Bishop Martin, those who removed the pulpit were just as guilty as those who installed it without the approval of the congregation. In an effort to calm the community, he and the other ministers organized a committee to officially investigate the crime. But when the committee failed to find the guilty party, some people in the church accused the bishop of covering up the truth. Prior to the theft, they argued, Bishop Martin had made it clear that he was against the pulpit: "It came in; I don't know how; and I wish it would go out; I don't know how" (Martin and Martin 1985: 38).

Bishop Martin is remembered as being a strong, very capable leader with an attractive personality. He preached in German, speaking in a high voice. His sermons were interesting, captivating, logical, and enthusiastic (Hoover 1982: 25–26). The bishop was a successful farmer and well respected by people inside and outside the Mennonite community. He had 11 children with his first wife, Sarah, who died just prior to the pulpit incident. His second wife, Anna, bore three more children. Martin wore dark, very plain clothing and a wide-brimmed black hat. He was of average height, built on the stout side, and his face had a healthy, ruddy appearance. His eyes were light in color, heavily browed, and, according to one of his daughters, always seemed to be filled with tears.

It was Martin's personal style to resolve disputes in his congregation as peacefully as possible (Hoover 1982: 25–27). He directed his congregation to preserve their traditions and Anabaptist heritage, but never thought that new ideas and practices, such as the elevated pulpit, would ever seriously disturb the harmony of the community (Weiler 1995: 21). Under his leadership, his church was the most conservative in the Lancaster Conference.

The bishop repeatedly expressed his disapproval of the pulpit theft and counseled members of the church to forget the episode.

Despite his attempt to close discussion of the incident, many people continued to complain and speculate about it. Seven or eight
men were expelled from the church because they refused to stop
bickering about the missing pulpit. Three or four others withdrew
their membership in response to the expulsions.

Over the next four years, with the intervention of ministers
from other Lancaster Conference congregations, some measure of
harmony was brought back into the congregation. The 11 men who
had been expelled or withdrew themselves were readmitted after
publicly acknowledging "that they did wrong by reaching back and
stirring up that that had once been settled by the church" (Wenger
1989: 23). In September 1893, Bishop Martin also admitted that he
had made a mistake by expelling the men so quickly.

A month after acknowledging his mistake, four years after the
pulpit was stolen, Bishop Jonas Martin, joined by his conservative
followers, formally broke away from the Lancaster Conference of
Mennonites. In Benowitz's judgment, this resulted in "the most significant of Mennonite schisms" (1996: 10). A contemporary Weaverland Mennonite justifies the need for the separation as follows:

> It was October 6, 1893, when Bishop Martin withdrew
> and started his own group. This seemed to bring better
> harmony among his followers than there had been for
> quite some time. In this way they could adhere to a more
> simple life style, and as before they tried to keep Christ
> and the scriptures central. (Wise and Martin 1990: 4)

Martin became the first bishop of the new Weaverland Conference of Old Order Mennonites. During his lifetime, he would
help establish 11 congregations. Today, the adult members of the
Weaverland Conference number approximately 5,000. There are
currently 30 churches located in Pennsylvania, Virginia, Missouri,
Wisconsin, Iowa, and New York.

Though it was a powerful symbol of conflict for many years, the schism in Lancaster would probably have happened without the pulpit incident. The great period of religious revivals and awakenings that swept through the United States in the nineteenth century had a profound impact on Mennonites. Progressive Mennonites believed that their church had lost its salt and fallen asleep. They were interested in rejuvenating the individual believer's relationship to his or her God. Following the example of other Protestant denominations, progressive Mennonites wanted people to become active missionaries in the world, spreading the Good News and winning souls. These Mennonites pressed for practical changes in their church: better trained preachers, English sermons, higher education for members, Sunday Schools, revival meetings, new hymnals, and more evangelical songs.

Conservative Mennonites, in contrast, resisted calls for change, arguing that imitation of the "high," worldly churches would lead members away from traditional concerns for community, humility, and simplicity. Bishop Jacob Wisler, for example, strongly advocated against instituting Sunday Schools. He led an initial reactionary schism in 1872, which established the Indiana/Ohio Old Order Conference of Mennonites. With regard to using an elevated pulpit, Wisler declared that he would rather preach from a hole in the ground (Weiler 1995: 23).

In 1889, old-fashioned Mennonites in Canada initiated a break from their progressive brethren and associated themselves with Bishop Wisler's group. They objected to revival meetings and were suspicious of the emotional conversions that often resulted from them. A final schism took place in Virginia, once again revolving around the institution of Sunday School. In 1901, this conservative faction joined Bishop Jonas H. Martin's Weaverland Conference of Old Order Mennonites.

In an attempt to clarify why there have been so many schisms among Mennonites, an Old Order minister told me the following story:

A Protestant preacher came to visit a Mennonite church one Sunday. He came because he had heard of our non-resistance (pacifism) and wanted to learn more about that. Well, that Sunday the (two Mennonite) ministers had a disagreement about the use of rubber tractor wheels. The one said they're fine, and the other said they're too worldly for Christians to use. So one of the ministers took half the congregation and separated from the church. After that, the visiting preacher shook his head and said "Now I know what non-resistance does for a church. Instead of arguing together until one side gives in, the factions just split away for good."

Jonas Martin and his followers refused to give in to the more progressive faction of Lancaster Mennonites. He took his stand and was resolute:

I am also in one with the old ground and council, but not with the new things that have been introduced. Giving together into marriage such that are outside of the church and with the Sunday Schools that are not held in peace nor with those that have made it thus am I not at one. If something is passed that is not good, one can change it again, one needs not to let it so. I have for a long time already agreed to these things against my conscience and I want to continue no longer in this or keep house this way. (Weiler 1995: 29)

In response, the seven bishops of the Lancaster Conference unanimously agreed to expel the conservatives from their church. In a statement read to a packed audience of church members, the bishops made the following proclamation:

The Savior says, "that he that is not with Me is against Me." We, as Bishops agreed that as he was so determined to stand against Conference there was no other remedy left for us in the Scripture but to deal with him as a transgressor and expel him from Conference, and he is no longer a member of the Mennonite Church that holds to the Lancaster Conference. . . . Consequently he has no right to preach and baptize according to the rules of the church. (Wenger 1989: 28)

Jonas Martin was not present during that fateful Sunday service, on October 15, 1893, when the bishops of Lancaster Conference formally excommunicated him. He was not far away, in the midst of a crowd of people who apparently shared his views: ministers, deacons, and approximately one-third of the Mennonites in the Lancaster Conference. He baptized 22 new members that morning.

The Origins of Mennonites in Europe and Their Migration to the New World

The various Mennonite churches that exist today grew out of a Christian movement originally known as *die Brueder* (the Brethren) or *die Wiedertaeufer* (the Anabaptists). The movement emerged in the early 1500s as a radical wing of the Protestant Reformation in Europe. In 1527, Anabaptists from Switzerland and Southern Germany adopted seven theological points, codified in the "Articles of Schleitheim." With this code, members of the group differentiated themselves from other religious groups, publicly explained their beliefs to outsiders, and attempted to authenticate a new "reason for being" (see Dyck 1981: 56–60). Although many different splinter groups have since developed out of the movement, the "Articles of Schleitheim" still provide the critical elements of a general Anabaptist creed. The seven points are:

1. The baptism of children is rejected (Antipedobaptism). Only adults are capable of understanding the spiritual meaning and implications of conversion and baptism.
2. Members of the church who do not conduct themselves as proper Christians will be encouraged to repent. Members who do not change their behavior will have the Ban (*Meidung*) imposed upon them. They will be denied fellowship with members until they repent and the Ban is lifted by the church leadership.
3. Communion will be served to members regularly. Those who partake will receive both wine and bread.
4. Members of the church must lead an existence that is distinctively set apart from the world (*Absonderung*). They are to be in the world but not of it.
5. The shepherds of the Church, the bishop and deacons, should be selected from the most respected married men of the congregation, according to the qualifications dictated by the Apostle Paul (*nach der Ordnung Pauli*, I Timothy: 3).
6. Violence in the name of justice is a concern for God alone. Christians should not be civil judges or soldiers; they must always lead peaceful lives.
7. Christians should not utter oaths of any kind.

The Reformation leaders Martin Luther and Ulrich Zwingli relied on the protection and cooperation of secular authorities in their struggle against the Roman Catholic Church. As the Anabaptists rejected the union of church and state, military service, and the swearing of oaths, they were commonly perceived as a threat to the established political powers. For this reason, members of the movement were severely persecuted by civil authorities and religious officials, both Protestant and Catholic. They were fined, imprisoned, executed, and sold into servitude. The Swiss cities of Zurich and Bern, for instance, issued numerous punitive mandates

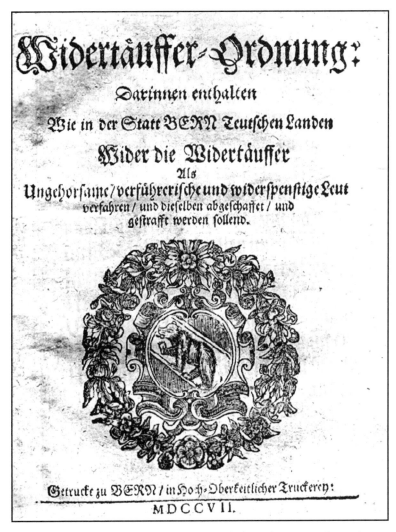

Figure 2.1. Attempting to halt the spread of Anabaptism, the Swiss city of Bern issued this mandate in 1695. The law compelled all citizens to swear loyalty to the established church. Anabaptists were expropriated, exiled, imprisoned, and executed. Many other cities issued similar decrees.

against the "disobedient, misleading, and rebellious" Anabaptists. Fleeing persecution, Anabaptists first attempted to escape danger by withdrawing out into the Swiss countryside, but migrations of greater distance followed into the Alsace-Lorraine, Northern Germany, Holland, parts of Eastern Europe, and eventually to Canada and the United States. Dutch Anabaptists under the leadership of Menno Simons (1492–1561), a former Catholic priest, were the first to be called "Mennonites."

William Penn, colonial governor of Pennsylvania, actively recruited Mennonites to settle in his colony, promising to guarantee their religious freedom. Economic opportunities in the New World also attracted Mennonites to leave Europe (Benowitz 1996: 4–5). The first permanent Mennonite community in America was established near Philadelphia in 1708, 15 miles northwest of Germantown. Colonial authorities provided the Mennonites with the best farmland available. Because the Mennonites were pacifists, they were generally granted land far away from hostile Native Americans. Scotch-Irish immigrants, in contrast, were strategically placed on the frontier.

During the first half of the 1700s, Mennonites struggled with the way they were perceived by other people. Other groups resented their favored political status, economic success, heretical religious convictions, Germanic culture, and social exclusiveness. According to Benowitz, Mennonite leaders urged members to practice a simple, nonconformist life-style in order to convince their British, Scotch, and Irish neighbors that they were not wealthy. (1996: 6)

Most of the ancestors of Weaverland Mennonites settled in the northeastern section of Lancaster County, Pennsylvania. By the time of the American Revolution, the steadily increasing population density in Lancaster County was already leading some Mennonite families to leave Pennsylvania. As they did in Europe, most Mennonites in the New World preferred the occupation of farming. A settlement was started in Virginia's fertile Shenandoah Valley in 1773.

After the Revolution, Mennonites who remained loyal to Great Britain emigrated to Ontario, Canada. Mennonites also moved westward into Ohio and Indiana and established very successful communities during the first half of the nineteenth century.

Migration of Weaverland Mennonites to New York State

In 1976, 12 families of the Weaverland Conference of Old Order Mennonites decided to migrate from Pennsylvania to New York State. In the course of 20 years, the Weaverland Mennonite community in New York State has grown to include approximately 110 households. Members have built two church buildings, three schools, and a fellowship center. Weaverland farms are widely dispersed across central New York, but most members live within 30 miles of the town of Seneca Falls (see figure 2.2).

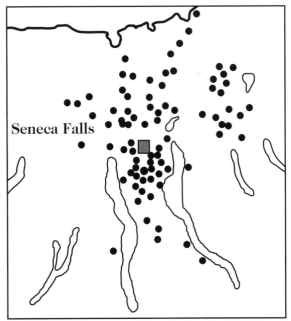

Figure 2.2. Weaverland Mennonite farms are dispersed around Seneca Falls, New York.

Weaverland Mennonites privately publish a membership directory that lists members according to family units (Wise and Martin 1990; 1995). The directory provided me with valuable demographic information concerning the church. Families are listed alphabetically by the father's last name. Each entry lists the names of the parents and children, along with the family's street address and phone number. Children who have formally joined the church but moved away from their parents are listed a second time, independently of their parents. The membership directory establishes links between generations and families by providing the names of grandparents, in-laws, and maiden names, along with birth, death, and marriage dates. The directory also lists the name of the particular Weaverland congregation to which a family belongs.

From the membership directory, it appears that Weaverland families in New York include about 475 children, with an average age of 12.5 years (Wise and Martin 1995). The average number of children per family is 4.3, with 40 families having at least six children. In 1990, the congregation numbered 67 households, 358 children, with an average number of 5.3 children per family (Wise and Martin 1990). These figures indicate strong population growth in the community, despite a reduction in the average family size. Not only are Mennonite families continuing to migrate into New York State, but also the congregation is successfully holding on to birthright members. Of children 18 years of age or older, it appears that only 5 percent did not join the church (8 out of 158).

Analyzing family entries in the membership directory reveals significant social differences between Weaverland congregations in New York and Pennsylvania. For instance, the average age of children and adults is much younger in the new settlement. In the Groffdale (Bareville, Pennsylvania) congregation, the average age of children is 36. In the Weaverland (Blue Ball, Pennsylvania) congregation, the average age of children is 38. In Pennsylvania, married children live in closer proximity to their parents. Mennonites in Pennsylvania seem to have a more difficult time keeping their children in the church. The Groffdale and Weaverland congregations, for example, appear to have lost 30 percent (163 out of 537) and 43 percent (156 out of 366) of children respectfully.

Both economic and religious interests motivated the Weaverland Mennonites who left Pennsylvania and migrated to New York. According to one member, "many of us shared the same concerns for lower priced farm land and a desire for a more rural life-style." On average, farm land in New York costs half as much as land in Pennsylvania and produces a comparable market value (USDA 1997). By buying farms in New York, Mennonites could continue in an occupation that was mutually compatible with their shared values. A Weaverland minister succinctly summarized the position of many of his peers when he recalled his own reason for joining the migration:

> It is very important for us to continue farming—our whole way of life depends on it. Without farms, the young men must take jobs away from home, out in the public works, where they are exposed to worldly ways. In Pennsylvania, only 5 percent of the church is still in farming. By coming to New York, nearly all members have been able to get back into agriculture.

Another member recalled the hope and optimism shared by the families that migrated:

> I wouldn't have moved my family up to New York if the others hadn't already gone. We heard that they were making it very well. . . . News came back all the time—about how cheap the land was and how quiet, much more peaceful than in Pennsylvania. The first families agreed to make the move together, building a new church. But after things went so well it was kind of like

a gold rush. Families were just racing to get up here.
There were empty farms all over, just for the taking.

Due to the depressed conditions of New York State's agricultural economy in the 1970s and 1980s, many native farmers were
happy to find Mennonites willing to take over their farms.

Note

1. *A Collection of Psalms and Hymns* 1977: 22.

Chapter 3

Social Life in the Community

Still on Thy holy Word
We'll live, and feed, and grow;
And still go on to know the Lord,
And practice what we know.[1]

The social life of Weaverland Conference Old Order Mennonites is strictly regulated by a normative code of behavior called the "Discipline," which is intended to protect the community's fundamental values. The Discipline, also known as the "Conference Rules," explicitly lays out standardized behaviors, prescriptive and proscriptive norms, with which members must conform or be expelled from the group. The Discipline, for example, prescribes what kind of automobile members may drive. All vehicles must be "in black color, [have] no stripes, nor [have] flashy trimmings" (Hoover 1982: 698). Because of their black vehicles, members of this church have been called "Black Bumper Mennonites."

Members claim that their adherence to the behavioral regulations of the church keeps them from becoming integrated with "the world." Working on Sundays, using a radio, watching television, joining political parties, wearing cosmetics, purchasing insurance policies, and driving sports cars are other things prohibited by the Discipline. In this chapter, I document significant aspects of group life among the Weaverland Mennonites and show how the Discipline creates visible uniformity in the group.

The Outward Appearance of Members

According to a member of the church, "The people of the world are too concerned with the things they wear, that they be pleasing to the sight and be in just the latest style. Such concern takes our minds away from where they ought to be." The clothing worn by Mennonites is designed to reflect simplicity. Through their uniformly styled dresses, for instance, female members demonstrate that they are "not part of the world and its fads." Head "coverings" are worn "to show the Angels that we are Christian women." "She should wear it constantly because the Angels are always present. She needs their protection all the time. They respect the veiled woman because this shows her voluntary submission as a godly woman" (*Home Messenger* 1994: 8). Men wear black straw or felt hats to all church events and when visiting friends and family on Sundays. Women typically sew their dresses and some of their children's clothing, though men's apparel is generally bought at "Plain Clothing Stores" located in Pennsylvania or through their mail-order catalogs. Jewelry is not worn by Mennonites, who consider it to be vain and "without a purpose."

Hair is worn by both sexes in strict conformity. Women's hair, which is always covered in public, must never be cut, curled, styled, or colored. "Women are to let their hair grow naturally as long as God allows it to grow" (*Home Messenger* 1994: 9). However, some women do admit to trimming the ends of their hair so that they are of equal length. Girls wear their hair in two long braids, straightly parted, and uncovered. Before being baptized as members in the church, which occurs at about 14 years of age, older girls "practice" wearing head coverings for about a year. One 13-year-old who had just begun practicing demonstrated to me how the "cap" is put on:

> You part your hair in the middle first and then you take the right side, wrapping it around your hand until you can put a bundle into the cap. Then the left side goes in and you pin it down. Then you carefully comb in the part at the back, leaving a tight part right down the middle. The [hair] ends get pinned under the cap. It takes practice!

Men and boys demonstrate a remarkable informal conformity in wearing their hair, which is usually cut by their wives or mothers. "They are to shear their hair, and it is a shame for them to let it grow long" (*Home Messenger* 1994: 9). Out of an assembled group of 27 male members, I once observed that 26 parted their short hair on the left side, with the remaining person parting his on the right. All 27 parts were very straight and long, wrapping far around the back of each head. Men and boys tend to use hair spray and water to hold their hair tightly in place. Nearly every male keeps a small black comb in his rear hip pocket.

The "plain" and undifferentiated quality of Mennonite apparel is well illustrated in the mail-order catalogs from which members purchase their clothing. There is no "Plain Clothing Store" in New York State, so members tend to order goods from the stores they frequented back in Pennsylvania. Items are presented in black and white photographs or pencil sketches, without models or backdrops. One company has a catalog that is more than 100 pages long; two pages are devoted to black shoe polish and leather soap, three pages to "hair accessories," 20 pages to sewing supplies, one and a half pages for "bra extenders" and garter belts. The selection of rubber work boots is twice as large as the selection of women's shoes. "Plain Clothing" catalogs tend to market their wares as "no nonsense," lacking frills, long lasting, and economical.

Mennonites seem to own three different categories of clothing, appropriate for three different kinds of social events: church, work, and visiting. The most traditional and finest clothing is worn to church on Sundays and is described in the next chapter. While on their farms during the week, Mennonite men wear plain durable work clothes. Short-sleeved cotton-blend shirts, with buttons and a single pocket, are standard. Dark blue, brown, or green work trousers are popular, as are plastic baseball caps, preferably without printed logos. Women tend to wear old church dresses, with the sleeves cut off in summer. They may wear tennis shoes and white socks for working around the house and garden. Women wear "cape dresses" of a uniform style, with inverted triangular panels covering the chest and back. The dresses are cut just below the knee. Girls tend to wear traditional dresses sewn by their older sisters or mothers. Boys wear the same clothing worn by most non-Mennonites.

The third category of clothing is worn when members visit friends or attend "singings" and other social events, such as the auction or farm sale. On these occasions, men usually wear dark blue trousers with blue and white-checkered shirts and women wear nylon print dresses with black or white stockings. According to one member of the church, "Married women are not expected to wear white stockings, however, it may be that they sometimes do. It is frowned upon by the Church. The Sisters are never expected to go into public without a cape dress."

Weaverland Mennonites are generally healthy-looking people. Obesity does not seem to be a problem for any of the male members, perhaps due to the amount of physical labor required in agriculture. Most of the women become rather stout after having their first child. One member reported that the last time she visited her obstetrician, he rudely told her that she must stop eating so much: "You Mennonites just eat pies and cakes." This woman eventually became the community's midwife.

Both men and women appear to age quickly. Couples marry young, usually between 18 and 21, and immediately start having children. Large families with five or more children are most common, which may have an effect on the outward appearance of parents, who often look worn out. Mennonite men have large strong hands, characterized by many creases, scars, and cracks that seem permanently filled with dirt and grease. The men scrub their bodies with soap and water before going to church, but some claim that their hands are impossible to clean. The smell of the cow barn or hog pen is extremely difficult to remove from their bodies.

Economic Activities

Nearly all members of the Weaverland community work in occupations related to agriculture, particularly the dairy sector. Several members raise hogs and one supervises a large fruit tree orchard. Members are not permitted to "buy and sell cattle," making a business as dealers in livestock. "When you get into that it's too tempting to tell stories about this or that cow that just aren't true. You have pressure to sell bad animals, and that puts you in a dangerous position."

Mennonite dairy farms in New York State are usually between 150 and 200 acres in size, with herds ranging from 35 to 100 milk cows. In addition, families typically raise calves to sustain the size of their dairy herd. Most members successfully grow the feed required for their herds, although high protein supplements formulated for dairy cows are purchased. Producing cash crops does not seem to have a strong appeal among the Mennonites in New York.

Selling milk on the open market for cash, Mennonite dairies are impacted by conditions affecting the greater economy of New York State. Milk is New York's primary agricultural product, worth almost $2 billion annually. Nearly all milk produced in New York is fed back to calves, while the remainder is consumed fresh or used to produce butter, cheese, and ice cream. Due to the increased use of special feed mixes and hormonal treatments, New York's dairy herd is becoming smaller but actually producing more milk. In 1989, for instance, the average cow produced 14,397 pounds of milk. There were 769,000 milk cows. In 1998, the average cow produced 16,748 pounds, with a herd of only 700,000.

One of the most significant changes in the state's dairy industry is the dramatically increasing size of individual herds. In the words of one Mennonite farmer, "You gotta get big or get out." Between 1989 and 1998, the total number of dairies fell from 13,500 to 8,700. During the same period, the number of dairies with fewer than 49 cows declined by nearly half. The number of dairies with between 50 and 199 cows declined 36 percent. As the total population of cows in New York declines, the size of individual herds is growing. There are now more than 500 milk cow operations with more than 200 cows (USDA 1997). Between 1964 and 1997, the number of New York farms with more that 2,000 acres nearly tripled, while the total land used by farms substantially decreased. These statistics describe the growing impact of large agricultural corporations, with their concentrated capital resources, heavier machinery, and advanced agricultural technology. As they struggle to survive in a competitive market, the pressures on small farmers in New York, particularly those who value a simple life-style, are severe.

The agricultural economy of New York was depressed throughout the 1990s, with approximately 40 percent of all farmers routinely claiming net losses. Milk prices in 1999 fluctuated unpredictably and fell to a historic low point. According to a Mennonite farm woman, "as the value of our milk falls year by year, the price for milk in the store increases." According to a comparative study by researchers at Cornell University, "New York dairy farmers milked nearly twice as many cows as their Canadian counterparts, but made substantially less money. . . . As a result, 10 times as many New York dairy farmers said they planned to quit farming" (*Herald American* 1994). The economic problems experienced by small farmers throughout the United States have been recognized by the United States Department of Agriculture, which commissioned a special task force to monitor and help relieve the plight of small farmers (USDA 1999).

Despite the fact that the New York dairy economy is suffering, Mennonite farmers seem to be relatively at ease. As one member told me:

> I can't complain about my situation. We bought a failed
> farm when we came up here and managed to turn it
> around. The slump allowed us all to buy the farms we
> came to. You can be sure that it's not the slow economy— the falling milk prices—that drive New York farmers into bankruptcy. We are doing fine, with a few exceptions. It's not the so-called high cost of living, but the cost of living high. We keep things simple, that's the key.
> And the Wengers—the horse and buggy people—are still
> coming up here [to New York] because they are even less
> concerned with living high.

Mennonite farmers tend to owe a great deal of debt on their farms to local banks. Debt, however, is not necessarily considered a bad thing to have. A member who is considered to be successful by his peers spoke of the need to go into debt:

> Everyone starting out in farming is going to have to borrow. If you can't get money from your Dad or other members then you have to go to the bank. The mistake many farmers make is that they never borrow enough money.
>
> You just can't make it with a small herd of 25—even if it feels good to owe less. If you have that many, you're going to work your tail off just to make the payments— when you retire you'll still be in the hole. You've got to have a herd of 50 or 60 or more—you just can't earn the money without those cows. They'll keep you busier than you like, but at least they'll eventually pull you out of debt. As for me, you know, I hate my cows.

After working on the farms of relatives for many years, one Weaverland family left Pennsylvania and bought a farm in New York with a barn capable of holding 54 cows. "This was our own farm, a dream come true. This spring after son Raymond came home, we began building a free stall barn for more than 100 cows and a flat barn parlor. We are presently milking over 80 cows with only four milkers, so we spend lots of time in the barn, anxiously awaiting the new improvements."

According to one of the first members to migrate to New York State, "Each farmer was, and still is, responsible for his own debt. It took great stewardship and management to make the investment work." Mennonite farmers have helped one another survive by sharing enterprising business skills, family labor, and community resources.

The entire family accomplishes work on the farm, with each child performing his or her chores. Most families tend to observe the same basic division of labor. While the men and boys operate the dairy, the women and girls cook, wash clothing, and clean the house. In addition, they are primarily responsible for yard work and tending the vegetable garden. The garden requires a tremendous amount of time in late summer and fall, when produce must be harvested. At peak season, it is common for the older children to operate a roadside fruit stand or greenhouse in front of the house. Great quantities of fruits and vegetables are canned, frozen, or bottled for use during the year. For example, a mother might can between 200 and 400 quarts of peaches annually.

The female members of the family always prepare meals. Supper usually consists of meat and several carbohydrate foods, such as potatoes, bread, homemade noodles, or corn. Canned fruits and vegetables accompany most major meals. Homemade catsup, pickles, and chow-chow (a relish of chopped pickles) are popular condiments. Water and milk are the usual beverages. There is almost always a dessert after the main meal: ice cream, apple pie, or chocolate chip cookies. As one older child claimed, "We couldn't do without dessert." Dinner is frequently served to each family member in a plain plastic bowl, from which all food is eaten. Before eating, the father leads a silent prayer of thanks. When the meal is finished, the women clear away the dirty dishes. I offered to help wash dishes once and was told by the man of the house, "Men don't do that here."

In the typical Old Order Mennonite family the mother is primarily responsible for the care of young children and babies. However, she depends on the support of her husband, older children, and relatives. Older sisters are especially apt to supervise their younger siblings. Since most farm work is accomplished close to home, children and working adults are almost always in one another's company. In order to take along a toddler, for instance, fathers add a small seat to their tractors. The presence of children in the barn, milking parlor, and around functioning machines occasionally results in serious work-related accidents. Mennonites seem to

accept such danger as an unfortunate but normal part of their agricultural life-style. For instance, one farmer was baling hay one late
summer. His five-year-old daughter was riding along with him on
the tractor when she fell off and was crushed. According to the
county sheriff who investigated the death, the farmer stopped the
tractor, carried his daughter's body inside the house, and laid her
on the floor. He told his wife that there was not anything else he
could do. Then he went back out to his tractor and continued to
bale hay (*Post-Standard* Sept. 3, 1996). A member of the church
explained that the girl "loved the field, and she wanted to be with
her father in the field." "I think everyone would feel it was supposed to happen according to God's plan," concluded another
member of the community. Whatever the risks, children quickly
learn how to be useful by watching their parents work. Child labor
contributes significantly to the economic success of farms.

As children mature, they may look for jobs away from home.
Daughters work in hospitals, geriatric centers, nurseries, and gro-
cery stores. If he is not needed at home, it is common for a young
man to work on another member's farm. After he gets married, a
man might work for an established farmer in exchange for a house
and modest income, perhaps 10 percent of the monthly milk
check. It is also common for an established farmer to purchase a
farm and dairy herd for a young couple, after which proceeds are
shared equally.

The "Protestant work ethic" characterized by the German
sociologist Max Weber (1988) well describes the Mennonite economic orientation.[2] Members report working up to 80 hours a week
on their farms. Families take few vacations because of the need to
milk twice daily. Money is not wasted on luxury items, status symbols, expensive vacations, and personal entertainment. Consistent
with the adage, "Idle hands are the devil's workshop," a member
told me that he would continue harvesting a field of rotten and use-
less hay just to keep working. "It's not the money that is important,
we need to be diligent in our labors for the glory of God. That is
what God expects from us."

Economics, for Mennonites, seems to be a form of worship that is accomplished in a spirit of separation from the world. Members pay income taxes to the state, but normally refuse federal and state farm subsidies and Social Security benefits. As the bishop once stated, "there is no such thing as security in the world." If a member's farm is threatened by bankruptcy, the ministry will appoint another member to take charge of the finances. Funds from the church may be used to help pull the farm out of trouble.

So that they are not "yoked" with the world, members of the church do not purchase insurance from "worldly companies." Instead, the Weaverland Conference has independently organized a very effective insurance system. The head of each household may elect to insure his entire farm and all of his family's equipment (tractors, implements, heavy machines, etc.), or he may opt to insure each building separately. In either case, he assesses the value of his property and informs the church how much insurance protection he requires. The amount he requests is eventually used to determine the premium he will have to contribute.

If damages are incurred by one of the members, a group of appraisers is sent out to inspect the insured property:

> The local Deacon selects one person as an appraiser and the owner with the loss selects another. The Deacon and the two appointees then calculate the damage and decide what the payment should be. The payment never may exceed the amount the owner had previously assigned to the property or building. . . . The amount to be collected will be announced at the Church services and the rate of collection is also announced.

Depending on the extent of the damages, the committee recommends that the entire Weaverland Conference take a collection "at a certain rate," specified as a certain number of "mil." This means that the head of each family must multiply the amount for which his property is insured by the recommended number of mil.

For example, if a family's own farm is insured for $100,000 and the church decides to collect "one mil," then the head of the house multiplies 100,000 by .001 to figure out how much his family should contribute to the collection. In this example, of course, the family would contribute $100 to the insurance fund. Most of the time, the committee recommends that the church raise "a half mil" (members multiply by .0005). Sometimes it occurs that no losses are claimed in a year. However, most families can expect to contribute $200 or $300 dollars annually to the insurance fund. This amount of money is but a small fraction of what "worldly" New York farmers pay to insure their property.

The extent of the insured family's loss and the number of mil required to repair the damages is announced at the end of worship service in all of the Weaverland Conference churches by the presiding deacon. He also announces the names of four local members who will travel around the area in the coming week collecting contributions, each man visiting all of the farms in a given direction: "Henry Martin will take the North, John Zimmermann will go East," and so on. "If a person has a substantially greater loss than is covered by his current assessment he is at liberty to ask the Deacon to announce the amount. If anyone wishes, they can increase their required contribution."

As do the Old Order Amish, Weaverland Mennonites help rebuild one another's homes and barns, which decreases reconstruction costs. On such occasions, the men of the congregation cooperate to repair structures, the women prepare and serve meals and refreshments, while the children watch the event and enjoy one another's company.

Weaverland Mennonites have created an effective insurance scheme to protect their automobiles. Members of the Conference originally established a bond of $1 million, secured at a "worldly" bank in Pennsylvania. Money is taken from this fund to pay losses when they are claimed, but it is replaced by premiums collected from members. Adequate liability insurance for one vehicle costs

$108 per year. Families that wish to purchase collision insurance to cover possible damages to their own vehicles pay an additional $108 for a supplemental policy, along with 5 percent of the estimated value of their car, paid in the first year only. In other words, the regular annual premium for a fully insured vehicle totals $216. A member reported to me that the cost of automobile insurance has not increased as long as he can remember. The system works so well that money raised from premiums is accumulating at the bank. Consequently, the membership has elected to stop collecting premiums from some members, including all of the widows and ministers.

Within reasonable limits, families are expected to pay their own medical bills. When a family cannot afford to pay all of their bills, the church raises money to cover the remaining cost of medical treatment. Old Order Mennonites make limited use of public health services, using them for occasional check-ups and immunizations. When they consider it necessary, members of the church do not hesitate to seek the advice of worldly physicians. A Mennonite midwife, who collects a small monetary fee or accepts barter goods, provides prenatal care and midwifery services to most mothers. For example, the midwife recently received a set of oak dining chairs, handmade by a father in exchange for her assistance. A few mothers prefer to give birth in local hospitals. If necessary, elderly members are taken care of in a residential home operated by the Conference. When they die, members are buried in a cemetery next to the church building, in graves marked by small, plain marble headstones.

School

In accordance with New York State law, all Mennonite children attend school, at least until the age of 14, when they begin to work at home until they marry. Girls tend to marry at about 18 years of age, while boys tend to marry at a year or two older. Until they turn

Figure 3.1. Most Weaverland children attend one of the three elementary schools operated by the community.

16, children are supposed to continue their education at home. State authorities require children to keep a record of their home schooling progress. In fact, this is rarely done and parents typically do not supervise the home schooling of their older children. The Old Order Mennonite community does not value higher education, which is considered a "worldly pursuit." "For the wisdom of this world is foolishness with God" (I Corinthians 3: 19).

The ministry of the church advises parents to send their children to one of the three schools operated by the church. Two of the school buildings have two rooms and enroll 40 students each. The third school building has three rooms for 60 children. The ratio of teachers to students is one to 20. Teachers are generally young single women who remain in the position until they marry. When asked if the teachers were recruited because they had themselves been good students, a mother and father of four school-age children shook their heads and grinned: "Not really. In Pennsylvania it was different, but . . . up here, on the farms, there just isn't enough work for the older girls to do. If a girl ends up teaching, it is probably because there isn't anything else for her to do."

Each family with children in the church school is required to pay about $1,200 tuition each year, regardless of how many children attend. The school board is comprised of three elected members and one supervising minister. The church ministry has authority over the education of the community's children. Religious training does not normally occur at school, as it is assumed that parents take this responsibility upon themselves in the home. Not all of the Weaverland families in New York State can send their children to a church school; for example, those who live on farms too far away. Consequently, some children go to public elementary schools. Many parents who send their children to public schools voice concern that their children will learn bad habits and "rebellious behavior" from the other pupils. It is certain that a more traditional style of discipline is maintained in the parochial school. In a book commonly consulted by Old Order teachers whom I interviewed, *Handbook for Creative Teaching* (Martin 1986), corporal punishment is recommended as the disciplinary method of choice: "There is something judicial and dignified about taking a child aside and giving him the standard remedy" (p. 679). In the next paragraph, the author of the book discusses the best instrument for spanking:

> The Bible says "rod." We generally think of a rod as something light, that stings but does not take a strong arm to make it effective, and which in the strong hands of a sensible person will not injure more than giving a mild bruising. A paddle with a lot of holes drilled in it to make it light and swift, can serve much the same purpose. A strap or short length of hose can work well, though some kinds are a little heavy. A plastic jump rope is light, but it stings. If you use one, by all means double it up; do not let it fly loose and wrap part-way around the student. (p. 682)

If a child gets into trouble at school, it is likely that his or her siblings will bring up the incident at the dinner table. With brothers and sisters in the same classroom, problems at school quickly become problems at home.

In the following interview, I questioned an adult member about leaving school and the value of higher education:

> MEMBER: The day after I turned 14 I walked up to my teacher's desk and put down my books. Told her I wouldn't be coming back. That was the first week of the ninth grade. She didn't believe me.
>
> AUTHOR: Were you glad to leave?
>
> M: Oh, yeah! I worked full time on the farm, my dad needed my help. At 16 I started working on a masonry team, afterwards on some different farms as a hired hand. I married at 21. . . with $20,000 in my bank account—since I had been working since I was 14.
>
> A: Do you ever wish that you had stayed longer in school?
>
> M: No. I kept learning about my occupation—about farming. My wife also quit after the eighth grade. . . . That is the Mennonite way. I don't think I needed any higher education. It really depends on how well you can learn by yourself.
>
> A: Can you think of any way the Mennonite community might benefit if some members did stay in school for higher degrees or specialized training? For example, how would it be if you had a Mennonite veterinarian?
>
> M: Well, I don't know how that would work, since most of us farmers tend to our own animals. . . . I can think of a good example, though. I have a friend (in the church) who does electrical work. I like him a lot . . . but, he isn't a very good electrician. After he works at my place he charges me about the same as a commercial electrician—somebody that had special training in school. If he is going to charge me that much, than he should have better stayed in school longer. He could really use the higher training. I guess we could benefit if some members had higher training.

Whether service and skilled labor exchanged between members is qualitatively better or worse than that supplied by professionals, Mennonites certainly value mutual assistance. Getting help from "unschooled" friends in the church is intrinsically attractive because it does not involve interaction with people outside the community. Though professionals might do better work, doing business with outsiders is considered risky because they do not subscribe to the practices of the church. The church, of course, could not discipline a dishonest outsider.

Entertainment Events

Members of the community do not place an especially high priority on entertainment. However, there are certain social events that members enjoy participating in when they can afford the time.

When they are not working, Mennonites tend to relax inside the house. Families play card and board games and make handcrafts. Without television and radio to occupy them, most Mennonites are voracious readers of books and magazines. Families typically subscribe to Old Order periodicals such as *Family Life*, *Young Companion*, and *Blackboard Bulletin*. Two popular weekly newspapers, *The Budget* and *Die Botschaft*, consist almost entirely of letters sent in by faithful readers. "Scribes" report about local weather conditions; the progress of crops and farm animals; visitors at last week's church services; and local births, engagements, marriages, and deaths. Scribes also relate to readers, in vivid detail, unlucky accidents. Here are four typical examples (personal names have been altered):

> Jonas Miller had a tragic experience when he got his hand in the log splitter, cutting off all four fingers behind the knuckles. It was –30 degrees so having a cold hand was in his favor. It didn't bleed much and didn't have pain till on the way to the hospital.

> Samuel, a 15-year-old son of Leon and Lena Burkholder, had an unpleasant experience while walking through

the haymow. His wet boots slipped and he fell against a post, breaking his nose and smashing his upper lip into his braces.

One-year-old Martha, daughter of Lee Roy and Vera Mae Kurtz, pinched her index finger in the playpen at the sewing last Tue. The nail and tip of her finger came off, exposing the bone.

Amos Hurst was building a birdhouse on Sat., when his left hand got in the table saw. One finger was cut off at the 2nd knuckle, the next finger was missed, the 3rd one chewed up, and the little finger slit lengthwise. He was taken to surgery for repairs.

Old issues of such periodicals are kept for years and read over and over again. Many children and adults also nurture relationships with pen pals who belong to distant congregations.

Mennonites especially enjoy spending time together as a community. On special occasions, such as weddings and family reunions, members meet at the Finger Lakes Fellowship Center. The building has a kitchen and can accommodate 300 people in the dining hall. Any member may rent the building, which costs $300 per day: "Nobody makes a profit. We all own the building together and the money just pays expenses." Flowers are planted in one corner of the center's lawn, with a short split-log fence forming a backdrop. The attractive corner is a favorite setting for taking wedding photographs. On his wedding day, a groom is caught by his best friends and playfully cast over the fence. "He is now on the other side of life and has to act like it." The bride is lifted up by her maids and shaken upside down to "get out the mischief."

Apart from special social occasions, Mennonites regularly visit one another's farms. Nearly every home has a special bedroom reserved for guests, the most elaborately furnished room of all.

Figure 3.2. Members meet at the Fellowship Center to celebrate weddings, reunions, and other community events.

Visitors can generally drop in without an invitation. When friends or family stop in, work on the farm is interrupted and the company is entertained. The men seem to most enjoy discussing the growth of their crops, the weather, and recently attended farm sales. Women—hosts and guests—tend to gather in the kitchen to socialize and prepare a meal. Young children play in the yard or house together, but older children prefer to separate into discussion groups of the same sex.

A "singing" is a special kind of visit, involving many different families who gather to sing hymns. Singings are usually spontaneously planned after Sunday worship service, and held the same evening after supper at a member's home. In the living room of the host's house, members sit in sections according to the part they sing: soprano, alto, tenor, and bass. Men and women sit opposite each other and take turns calling out the page numbers of favorite songs. The hymnals used at singings are different from those used in church. They are larger in size, have musical notation, and include many traditional Protestant hymns. They would be considered inappropriate for use in worship. Members appear to really enjoy singing together at these events. At a singing, hymns are sung louder, faster, and with greater harmony. A dessert, such as ice cream or candied apples, is often served after the singing is over, while visiting continues.

Two other entertainment events also involve singing: "male
chorus" and "singing school." Male chorus is scheduled about every
three weeks and takes place in the workshop of one of the most tal-
ented songleaders. He cleans and hoses down the shop with water
before the event. Hymns are selected from a book especially for
Mennonite male choruses and sung in four-part harmony: first and
second tenor, baritone, and bass. The choral group is led by the
songleader, who moves his hand up and down to keep the tempo.

It is important to note that the men and boys who attend
male chorus are not there to practice singing; songs are never
rehearsed or worked at. Even if the song is poorly sung, the group
does not try to improve their performance. There may be two reasons for this. First, Old Order Mennonites are generally uncomfortable with showmanship and performing. Practicing might
detract from the spiritual value of the hymn, and encourage pride.
Second, not all of the members who attend male chorus come
because they want to sing. At the beginning of male chorus, which
is always held at night, many of the younger boys stand outside and
talk, smoking cigarettes and listening to rock and country music
played from cassette decks in their cars. Though the church pro-
hibits radios, cassette players are permitted. This "makes sense" to
members, because while tapes can be carefully selected, one cannot control what comes over the airwaves. After the first few songs
are sung without them, the younger boys come inside and join the
chorus.

One of the ministers explained that the boys are not questioned
about their smoking, though "it is not considered a normal and condoned practice. . . . Nobody likes what they do. But as long as they do
things like that with other boys from the church, we tolerate it.
Things would be worse if they did it with outsiders." The father of
several boys made the following remark with great emphasis:

> In our Church circles we have many young people who
> neither smoke or listen to rock music. Smoking and

rock music, among other impure practices, are strongly counseled against on Council Day. Many, many sermons are also directed against these impure practices. . . . Most of the parents I know are very concerned about their children's salvation and sincerely plead with them to accept the Lord and lead a God fearing life.

At the end of male chorus, which lasts an hour and 15 minutes, the songleader's wife and daughters bring dessert, soda, and juice into the shop. Participants visit for another half-hour before returning to their homes.

Every couple of weeks the young adults and older children will attend "singing school." This is organized by two of the church's songleaders and normally takes place Sunday afternoon at the church building. The young people attend singing school because they can spend time visiting together without the company of their parents, and because they enjoy singing their own songs. The youths learn yet another set of hymns and songs that are comparatively upbeat, often borrowed from more evangelistic churches.

The most popular form of entertainment for most Mennonite men is attending the weekly livestock auction. Even if they have no intention to buy or sell, members attend just to watch the sales and discuss cattle and the world. The auction is a spectacular event, drawing a wide variety of different people. The auctioneer sits in a booth above the square show pen. Men sit in cliques on three sides of the smoke-filled room: the Amish, the Wenger Mennonites, the Weaverland Mennonites, and the New York farmers forming their own separate sections. The auctioneer musically rattles off prices while animals are ushered in and out of the pen, prodded along with canes. Throughout the lively event, Mennonite men talk and enjoy each other's company.

In a film portraying the social life of the Old Order Amish, *Not To Be Modern* (1988), an Amish woman discussed the popularity of "sewing circles" and "quilting bees" within Mennonite communities. She claimed that while men have their fun at the auction, women prefer getting together to quilt and sew. Women in the Weaverland community produce most of the clothing worn by themselves and their children. Sewing is commonly viewed as hard work, but also it is esteemed as a means of expressing one's personality and Old Order identity. Asked about sewing, a member commented on why it was important to her:

> You know we have special clothing in our community that we just could not buy elsewhere. It is important for us to dress plainly, and by making our own dresses, we can get just the style we want in the right fabric. I make all of the girls' dresses, and, of course, mine too. It takes me about three hours to finish a dress for one of the girls. And mending torn clothing or replacing lost buttons saves a great deal [of money]. And I like to see the children dressed in my clothing.

One Weaverland family has opened a store that specializes in sewing supplies and bulk foods. At the store, women of the community can easily find bolts of fabric that would be considered appropriate for Old Order clothing. Women will often go to the store together with their friends and make a social event out of shopping.

At a sewing circle, several women or girls convene with their sewing machines at a member's home. While talking about their lives and enjoying one another's presence, members accomplish their individual sewing tasks in a social setting. Beginners especially benefit from the sewing circle by observing the skills of more experienced seamstresses and receiving their technical advice. Of course, participants in the sewing circle do not limit the topic of their discussion to making clothing. Members use the opportunity to talk about personal and family concerns, exchange gossip about other members, and to compare the behavior of their husbands and children.

Quilting is a traditional art widely practiced among Mennonite women. Beds are usually covered with beautiful handmade quilts during the day and the guest bed is often decorated with an especially elaborate quilt. After a woman cuts and assembles pieces of fabric for the top layer of the quilt, she may invite her family and friends to a quilting bee. At the quilting bee, the top pieced layer, the insulating batting, and the bottom fabric layer are sandwiched together and spread over a square wood frame. The quilting frame, as it is known, usually takes up most of the space in a family room and the women surround the frame as they quilt. With needles and thread, they carefully quilt the layers together using a running stitch. They follow a previously sketched pattern that marks the quilting design onto the top pieced layer. Quilting patterns, or templates, are often passed from mother to daughter over successive generations. Patterns are also traded among friends. While working on the quilt, women enjoy another opportunity to socialize. In addition to being a social activity, quilting can be a source of outside income. According to one member,

> There is a non-Mennonite woman down in Lancaster that makes a business selling quilts produced by Mennonites. We get between $100 and $200 for each quilt we make for her. She charges much more for the quilts. And she never seems to have enough!

> By selling her quilts to the businesswoman in Lancaster, this quilter earns about 25 cents an hour. When asked if she thought she was getting a fair wage, she matter-of-factly replied, "No. But, I'm here anyway."

Notes

1. *A Collection of Psalms and Hymns* 1977: 51.

2. Redekop, Ainlay, and Siemens (1995) critically evaluated Weber's understanding of Mennonites. Though Weber's specific portrayal of Men-

nonites might be superficial, I believe that his general characterization of the "Protestant worker" accurately describes Weaverland Mennonites. While the Old Order Mennonite wishes to live in isolation from the world (which puts him at odds with most capitalists), he believes that God has "called him" to a certain occupation; he avoids conspicuous consumption, values self-sufficiency and personal industry, and is suspicious of leisure.

Chapter 4

The Worship Service

Now is th' accepted time,
Now is the day of grace;
Now, sinners, come without delay,
And seek the Savior's face.[1]

Members of a typical Weaverland Mennonite family seem to move most quickly on Sunday mornings. Everyone in the community is expected to be at the church building when the worship services begin at 9:00. As on any morning, the cows need to be milked, and many other morning chores need to be taken care of. If possible, jobs are done in advance on Saturday evening in order to save time. The animals, for example, are fed twice what they normally get. The automobile is carefully washed. Shoes are shined, clothing is laid out, and food is prepared so that it can be warmed up for dinner after church.

As soon as they finish milking, members of the family rush into the house and get out of their "barn clothes," scrub themselves in the bathroom, and change into their best clothes. In a family of six or eight people, each person's shower must be short. When the polished family sits down at the kitchen table, the parents and children nod for a moment or two in silent gratitude, and then eat breakfast as fast as they can.

On the way to church, everybody seems to keep their eyes on the roads, searching for other black cars. The father, concerned with the clock, speeds along, accelerating with a punch and braking too quickly to swerve around corners. A child discovers an unidentified moving car and points a mile down the road. "Who is that? Over there!" "Must be the John Nolts," declares an older brother. "No, not the Johns," corrects the father, "that's the Gerald Nolts." As they come closer to the church building, the discoveries and recognitions become more frequent.

At the top of the last hill, there is a long, single story brick building. The features of the well-kept church are very simple, without any ornaments that might signify its religious function. The black cars stop in front of this building and take turns entering the parking lot. A continuous line of vehicles slowly curves from the road around to the back of the building. Each father stops first at the "women's door," waiting for the females in his family to get out of the car. Then the men and boys continue around the building to find an empty parking place. Thirty or 40 cars are neatly parked in a circle, all facing the same direction, toward the church.

After turning off their engines, the men and boys quietly sit in their automobiles for a few moments. After the older men begin to get out of their cars, the younger ones follow them. As they approach the "men's entrance," the men solemnly greet each other with handshakes and the kiss of peace. The women, on the other side of the building, also greet one another in this manner. The older boys do not immediately enter the church, preferring to visit in the parking lot as long as they can.

In conformity with the regulations of the church, the men wear black suits without lapels, and white shirts. Just inside the men's entrance, there are hooks on the wall for the men to hang up their black hats. Women wear long, solid-pastel colored cape dresses, cut in the same style, with white bonnets ("coverings"). They hang up their black overcapes, shawls, and heavy outer bonnets on hooks in the "women's wrap room."

When it is time to begin the service, the older men and women find their places on the benches, which are on opposite sides of the rectangular building. The rest of the membership, except the boys who are still outside, follow the elders into their pews. The men, women, young boys, and girls all sit in separate sections of the church.

At the front of the building, six men sit on two sides of a long table. They thumb through little black songbooks, quietly discussing songs that they might choose to sing. The man who has been a songleader the longest announces the number of the first hymn. "We will open this service by singing hymn number thirty-four." He then begins to sing out the song, assisted by the other men at the "singer's table." Members find a hymnal and flip to the right page, singing along.

Welcome, sweet day of rest,
    That saw the Lord arise;
Welcome to this reviving breast,
    And these rejoicing eyes.

The King Himself comes near,
    And feasts His saints to-day;
Here we may sit and see Him here,
    And love and praise and pray.

One day amidst the place
    Where my dear God hath been,
Is sweeter than ten thousand days
    Of pleasurable sin.

My willing soul would stay
    In such a frame as this,
And sit and sing herself away,
    To everlasting bliss.
                        (*A Collection of Psalms and Hymns* 1977: 34)

Songleaders always lead while sitting on their benches, without
keeping time with their hands.

In the middle of the first hymn, the ministry enters the building from the "anteroom." The bishop appears first, followed by the
preachers and the deacons. They take their seats on a bench in the
front of the building, along the wall behind the singer's table (see
figure 4.1).

When the first song is over, the songleaders turn their faces
and exchange glances with the ministry, who, in turn, calmly look
among themselves. Eventually, after consultation with his peers,
one of the ministers will recommend in a whisper to the deacon
that a particular hymn be sung. The deacon then announces the
page number of the song to the congregation. The deacon or one of

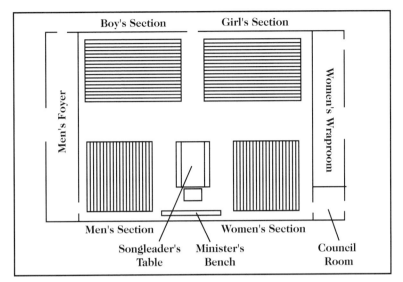

Figure 4.1. Sketch of the Interior Floor Plan of the Weaverland Mennonite Church Building

the ministers may then "line" the hymn, reading one or more of the verses aloud. When the lining is over, the number is repeated once more before one of the songleaders starts the hymn. A member of the church explained that the practice of "lining" is probably a practice "that started in old times when illiteracy rates were higher and there was a shortage of books." In fact, Bishop Jonas Martin may have initiated lining as a way to teach German to the children. After announcing a song, he would tell the children to "get a book and follow after" (Martin and Martin 1985: 70).

Sometime during the singing of the second hymn, the older boys enter the building from the back door. As on every Sunday, it is quite a dramatic ordeal when the boys come in late after talking in the parking lot. Throwing the double doors open with a bang, the boys march to their pews in a single-file line. Every other member, while continuing in his or her song, turns to watch the procession with reproach.

In this weekly "ritual of rebellion" (Gluckman 1954), the boys engage in overtly disruptive behavior, an activity that is usually denied them as individuals. When asked why the boys are not forced to enter the church on time, an older man said, "They'll grow up soon. The boys must be allowed to have their time of small rebellion." Another member commented: "The practice of the young boys coming into the church after the services have started is not something that we are proud of. However, it is difficult to change the habit after having tolerated it for many years. Many feel that it should not be."

At the end of the second hymn, one of the ministers stands and greets the assembly. He gives the first sermon, without notes, speaking for approximately 15 minutes. When finished, he asks the congregation to pray. In a sweeping collective movement, all members lean forward in their pews, pivot around on one bent leg, and assume a kneeling position. Eyes are closed and foreheads pressed tightly into the back support of the pew. After about two minutes of silence, the minister says "Amen," ending the prayer. Then the minister returns to the bench to sit down.

From his seat on the same bench, the second minister or bishop, whoever intends to give the second sermon, locates a chapter in the Bible upon which he will base his sermon. He leans over to the deacon and shows him the passage, giving him the book. The deacon rises and greets the congregation, admonishing them to listen to the reading of the scripture and the subsequent lesson. The deacon then reads the selected chapter to the group. When he is finished, he sits down and the second minister rises to the table.

For the next 15 minutes, the second sermon is much like the first in that it consists of a freely associated string of thoughts, Bible verses, and anecdotal illustrations. If a transcription of the sermon were cut into paragraphs, one who had not heard it might have a difficult time reassembling the parts. For the rest of his sermon, the minister will reread the selected chapter from the Bible, verse by verse, pausing between verses for commentary. The second sermon usually lasts between 25 and 30 minutes. When the sermon is over, the minister sits down.

One by one from their seats on the bench, the bishop, first minister, and deacon all give "testimonies" as to the usefulness and accuracy of the second sermon. Most of the time, they simply express agreement with what was said by saying something like, "We too can give a hearty amen and wish the blessings for the same." Sometimes another passage from the Bible will be read or illustration shared. Finally, after testimonies are made, the minister who delivered the main sermon will again rise to the table and express two things. First, he thankfully acknowledges the comments made by the others. Second, he maintains that "we should not be credited for anything good that might have been in our lesson, which could only have come from the Lord." If anything incorrect or bad was said, however, "it was due to our own human weakness and lack of knowledge." After the second minister acknowledges the testimonies and gives his disclaimer, he leads the congregation in a second kneeling prayer.

After the prayer, the congregation focuses attention on the songleaders, who look among themselves until one of them suggests a hymn. The suggestion is conveyed with a whisper to the bishop who is expected to confirm it. If the ministry positively confirms the hymn, the songleader who suggested it begins singing. When it is over, another hymn is suggested, confirmed, and sung. When this final hymn is over, the deacon stands and gives any necessary announcements about upcoming events, financial collections, or births and deaths.

When the deacon sits down, the minister who gave the second sermon stands and gives a benediction: "The grace of our Lord Jesus Christ, the love of God the Father, and the fellowship of the Holy Spirit, be with us all evermore. Amen." After the benediction, the congregation stands and listens to the bishop recite the "Lord's Prayer."

When the service is over, most members remain in and around the building to talk. This is a valuable time of spontaneous

Figure 4.2. After worship services, men line up their cars to pick up the women.

social interaction, as the entire congregation normally assembles only once a week. The men and women, boys and girls, visit amongst themselves, with only the youngest children freely mixing between the sexes. When it is time to leave, a father will collect his boys and drive the car around to the women's side of the building. The men patiently line up their cars to wait until they can pick up the women and girls in an orderly manner.

Older members suggested to me that the order of the Weaverland service has been much the same throughout their lifetime, though some changes have been made since Jonas Martin founded the conference. For instance, worship services are no longer conducted in German. The tempo of singing is slightly quicker, the selection of hymns is larger due to the inclusion of some mainstream Protestant hymns, and the normal worship event lasts about two hours, an hour less than it used to. The construction of the building and the arrangement of pews, singer's table, and the preacher's table is still basically the same as it was 100 years ago.

The members of the ministry, it should be noted, always speak in the plural when they are leading worship. They say, for example, "we would like the congregation to be attentive to the reading," or "we remember the story of a boy who was lost." One of the ministers explained the reason for using the plural form, "We speak so that we avoid the singular, the self. When we speak to the congregation, we do not do so through our own personal authority. It is the Holy Spirit speaking from within us."

The bishop, deacon, and ministers who supervise the congregation are not formally trained in theology and are expected to continue in their normal secular occupations. Church leaders who join "the ministry" are nominated for their respective positions and then selected by lot. Each male who joins the church must acknowledge his willingness to join the ministry if called to do so. A member described the process for nominating "a class" of brethren:

> The bishop first tells the congregation that a position needs to be filled. He asks them to give him recommendations. The recommendations are discussed by the ministry before going back before the whole congregation. Everyone is asked if there are any good reasons why this man or that man should not be fitting for a deacon or minister, whatever.

Once the members of the class have been individually approved to share the lot, a worship service is conducted during which the following procedure is used to select one person to fill the position:

> Then the bishop arises and gives a slip of paper, whereon is written, "The lot is cast into the lap but the whole disposing thereof is of the Lord" (Proverbs 16: 33). The slip of paper is given to the deacon to be placed into one of the books (identical German hymn books are used, one for each person participating in the lot).
> The ministers go into the counsel room, and after a short prayer, the home deacon places the slip of paper into one of the books while the other two deacons have their backs turned. Then each minister takes a turn to

shuffle the books so no one, except God, knows where the slip of paper is.

The bishop (in front of the assembled congregation) sets the books, one at a time, on the singers' table, in front of the class, in no set order, only as God guides his hands. After returning to his place behind the preachers' table, he admonishes the class to take their books; the one who arises first has first choice, and the last one takes what is left, although it is customary that they arise and choose by age.

After each has taken a book, the bishop begins looking for the slip, beginning with the book of the oldest in the class. The brother whose book contains the slip of paper is told to rise, and the bishop lays his hands on the brother's head and gives him his charge. He then gives him the kiss of peace and a few words of encouragement. (*COF* 1996: 66–67)

This method of selection is intended to allow God to have the decisive role in choosing leaders of the church.

In Upstate New York, Weaverland Mennonites worship in one of two church buildings, located in Fayette or Pleasant Ridge. For two consecutive Sundays, families attend the church nearest their farm. Every third Sunday, all of the members meet at the same building, which is alternated. This "three and one rhythm" is intended to sustain the familiarity of members who otherwise rarely see each other. Determining whether they must drive "up or down" on a given Sunday can be confusing for members, so the Conference publishes a special calendar booklet each year, currently in its 70th edition (*Mennonite Calendar* 2000).

Note

1. *A Collection of Psalms and Hymns* 1977: 25.

Chapter 5

Collective Rituals: Baptism, the Holy Communion, and Foot Washing

You call me Lord, and Master too,
*   Than do as I have done to you;*
All my commands and councils keep,
*   And show your love by washing feet.*[1]

Celebrated on the same day, two of the most important religious
rituals practiced by baptized members of the Weaverland Mennonite community are the Holy Communion and Washing of Feet.
"Holy Communion is commemorated twice a year, in the spring
and autumn, provided that the counsels and ministerial conference
feel there is sufficient unity" (*COF* 1996: 53). I attended normal
Sunday services more than a year before asking if I would be welcome at a communion service. Members enthusiastically encouraged me to attend.

   This chapter is a detailed description of members of the
church performing the rituals of baptism, communion, and foot
washing. Among my observations, I have interspersed relevant passages from the *Confession of Faith* booklet (*COF* 1996), which
explicitly prescribes how the rituals should be completed. While
precise directions are given in the *COF* for the procedures of each
ritual, *how* they must be performed and detailed accounts of the
"spiritual significance" of the actions—that is, *why* they are performed—are not provided. Part Two of the *COF* is entitled "Old
Order Mennonite Standards, Church Forms and Guidelines of the
Weaverland Conference Mennonite Churches." The origin of the
"guidelines" is explained in the Preface to Part Two of the *Confession of Faith*:

>   These Mennonite forms and guidelines were compiled
> by a committee and adopted by the Weaverland Confer-
> ence, on October 5, 1995. They were the result of prac-
> tices handed down to us for numerous generations.
> Also, much was taken from the second part of our for-
> mer booklet, which had been translated from a book
> (written in 1841) by Bishop Benjamin Eby of Ontario,
> Canada entitled *Kurz Gefasste Kirchen Geschichte*.
>
>   The publication of Part Two of this booklet brings the
> Pennsylvania Old Order standards and the Weaverland
> Conference forms nearer into focus than the older book-

lets which had a Canadian origin. It is our prayer that it
may bring honor to God and a blessing to the church.
(*COF* 1996: 37–38)

The communion service begins at 9:00 A.M., a half-hour earli-
er than normal Sunday services, and lasts for three and a half
hours, an hour longer than normal. The service is ordered much
like the usual worship service, except that a third sermon is given
by the bishop who presides over the ceremony, giving the sacra-
mental "emblems" to each baptized member. All three sermons follow a predictable pattern, closely adhering to prescribed biblical
texts. Foot washing is performed immediately after communion is
served.

Preparing for Communion: Introspection and Inspection

Weaverland Mennonites have organized a schedule of several congregational events to prepare for and then celebrate communion
and foot washing. The series of events begins during a normal Sunday service, at which the deacon is asked to read chapter 7, verses
1 to 14, from the Gospel of Matthew. This text is traditionally read
to remind members that no individual is without fault and that
they should not judge one another.

> The sermon is meant to turn the minds toward self-
> examination, counsel, and Communion, and the neces-
> sity of being on the narrow path that leads to eternal
> life. (*COF* 1996: 41)

Two weeks after the reading of this Scripture, a special Sunday service known as "Counsel Meeting" takes place. This meeting
proceeds in the same way as a normal service, except that "counsel" is given after the sermons, prayers, and singing.

> After the singing, the ministry will answer for themselves, confessing peace and a desire for Communion and Foot Washing. The ministry will then announce to the congregation that they will now go into the counsel room to receive their counsel. The sisters are to come first and then the brethren. (*COF* 1996: 42)

From the congregation assembled in the main room of the church, individual members may decide to enter the counsel room and speak privately with the ministers. This provides an opportunity for members to bring to the attention of the bishop, preachers, and deacon any personal or congregational problems that concern them. Generally, members will enter the counsel room in small groups of up to ten or twelve. It is rare for an individual to "seek counsel" alone.

> As they come into the counsel room, they are asked by the minister if they can confess peace, and have a desire for Communion, and are satisfied with the ministry and the church in general. (*COF* 1996: 42)

After members have been given the chance to seek counsel, the ministers return to the assembled congregation. The senior minister announces the counsels to the church. Then, he concludes the service with a benediction.

The sermons given at Counsel Meeting are intended to admonish the members to get spiritually ready for the coming communion. They are told that they must heal any broken relationships with other members, take inventory of their lives, and make sure that they confess all of their sins so that they are worthy of taking communion. The previous edition of the *Confession of Faith* booklet contains a section emphasizing that communion is a sacred event meant only for "prepared" individuals:

According to the evangelical teaching of Jesus and His apostles, the Holy Communion is an exclusive partaking by the true believers, by His own followers who belong to him. The unbelievers and wicked, as long as they persist in their impenitent condition, have nothing in common with, do not participate in the means of grace of the holy Communion, for according to the precepts of Paul no one who is unworthy of it shall partake of the Lord's Supper (I Cor. 11:29). (*COF* 1989: 47)

During the week after Counsel Meeting, the ministers from each local Weaverland Conference church meet together in Pennsylvania and hold "Conference Meeting." At this event, the ministers discuss the spiritual concerns that members may have conveyed to them in the Counsel Room during Counsel Meeting. The leaders of the Conference meet together in this way so that the local churches continue to operate in a uniform fashion. Ministers are also able to consult one another about how to deal with any significant problems in their particular church.

On the Saturday after the ministers return from Conference Meeting, the Weaverland Mennonites hold an event that they call "Preparatory Service."

This day is used for certain housekeeping duties such as almsgiving, and explaining church discipline by reading the conference report and the combined counsels of the churches. At times acknowledgments need to be made, and if there are applicants, the baptisms are performed on this day. (*COF* 1996: 46)

At this event, young people of about 15 years of age may be baptized and welcomed into the church as new members. Most baptisms occur in the Fall Preparatory Service, after the young people have attended "Instruction Meetings." During these meetings, which "begin the last Sunday afternoon in July at two o'clock," the young people "study" the First Part of the *Confession of Faith* booklet. The First Part of the little black paperback contains the Eighteen Articles of the Dortrecht Confession of Faith, adopted by Anabaptist ministers in 1632. At each meeting for instruction, three of the Articles are read aloud to the "applicants."

> Applicants will sit near the preachers' table, with the boys on the men's side and the girls on the women's side. The ministry come in the same door as the others. Services begin by singing two hymns, followed by a short, opening message by a minister, and then a kneeling, silent prayer. Three ministers will each teach one of the eighteen articles, followed by testimonies. The minister who taught last will lead in a kneeling, audible prayer, closing with two hymns and a benediction. (*COF* 1996: 45)

After the Ninth Article has been introduced, and once again at the last instruction meeting, the bishop asks the class "if they are satisfied with the teaching they have received." The last three Articles of the Dortrecht Confession are read "on a Friday afternoon at two o'clock," with only the applicants and the ministry in attendance. At this last meeting, the boys wear dark suits and the girls wear dark dresses, preferably navy blue.

In order to be baptized during the Preparatory Service, each individual applicant must have attended all of the Instruction Meetings and been approved by the congregation at the Counsel Meeting.

> Baptism is an outward testimony of an inner New Birth experience, and Baptism shall be administered upon a confession of one's faith and repentance toward God. (*COF* 1996: 47)

Wearing dark clothing, the applicants bow on their knees in front of the membership to make their three "baptismal vows." The complete vows, as pronounced by the bishop, are as follows:

The first question of the baptismal vows is: Do you believe in one almighty God who hath created heaven and earth—all things visible and invisible and preserves the same by His power; and do you believe in Christ Jesus, His only begotten Son, who was conceived of the Holy Spirit and born by the pure virgin Mary, suffered under Pontius Pilate, died on the cross, was buried in a sepulcher, arose victorious the third day, and after forty days ascended into heaven to the right hand of God, from whence he will come again to judge the living and the dead; and do you believe in the Holy Spirit who proceeds from the Father and the Son, to chasten the world because of sin, and that you have become willing to be baptized by the guidance of the same? Can you answer this with "Yes"?

Secondly, you are asked, are you sorry for your past sins and are you willing to renounce Satan and the dark kingdom of this world, your own will and all the satanical works of this world? Are you willing to be subject to the Gospel of Christ Jesus, to have the same rule in and over you as much as God grants you grace? Can you answer this with "Yes"?

Thirdly, are you willing to submit to the Gospel of Jesus Christ, especially Matthew the 18th Chapter, where it says, "If thy brother shall trespass against thee, go and tell him his fault between thee and him alone; if he shall hear thee thou hast gained thy brother, but if he will not hear thee, then take with thee one or two more that in

the mouth of two or three witnesses every word may be
established. And if he shall neglect to hear them, tell it
unto the church, let him be unto thee as a heathen man
and a publican"? Are you willing to have this used against
you and help use it against others as necessity may
demand? Can you answer "Yes"? (*COF* 1996: 49–50)

After the converts have affirmed these vows, the bishop
kneels with them in prayer, closing with a solo recital of the Lord's
Prayer. The bishop then rises and steps before each kneeling convert, one at a time, with his hands laid upon their uncovered heads
he says:

Upon thy confession of faith, which thou hast confessed
before God and many witnesses, thou art baptized with
water, in the name of the Father, and of the Son and of
the Holy Ghost. (*COF* 1996: 51)

When the bishop says the words, "baptized with water," to
each convert, the deacon pours a small amount of water on top of
the new member's head.

When all are baptized, the bishop then approaches the
first baptized person and extends him the right hand of
fellowship and says, "In the name of the Lord, in the
name of the church, I offer thee my hand; arise, to a new
beginning, to a new life. The Lord strengthen you that
you may be able to finish your newly started work, and
be his disciple; acknowledge the truth and the truth
shall make you free." (*COF* 1996: 51)

As a conclusive sign of acceptance, the bishop exchanges the
"kiss of peace" with each of his new brethren. The bishop's wife
greets each of the new sisters with the same sign. The new members

are then asked to be seated and the Preparatory Service continues to the end.

After Counsel Meeting and Preparatory Service, the actual communion service is held on a Sunday. In summary, the celebration of "Communion" consists of three distinct ritual events: Counsel Meeting, Preparatory Service, and Communion with Foot Washing. It would be abnormal for a member not to attend each of these events. It would be extremely unusual for a member to miss the communion service.

The Holy Communion

Since female members are dropped off at the women's entrance to the church building, I did not notice their total uniformity of color until I was seated opposite them in the main room. All of the women, about 75 of them, were wearing long black dresses. On normal Sundays, the women wear dresses of various pastel colors. On this communion day, the blackness of the women's section, combined with the usual blackness of the men's section, produced a stunning sensory effect. The two narrow ribbons attached to the women's white bonnets were also black, loosely hanging down their necks. The black dresses clearly indicated the special importance of this Sunday.

One of the songleaders opened the service with a hymn. That hymn was quickly followed by another. In the middle of the second hymn, many of the adults began to glance over at three empty pews where the older boys were supposed to be sitting. As I already related, it is normal for the boys to talk in the parking lot until the first or second song is started. After they "realize that worship has begun without them" they walk in late as a group. Even though they habitually stay outside too long, they always come in during one of the first two hymns. I did not expect the boys to delay on this special Sunday. As the second hymn ended, it seemed as if everyone was impatiently waiting for the boys to come in. Even the younger boys turned around to look at the empty pews.

> The first minister will teach, by memory, of the creation
> and the fall of man from Genesis 1 to 9:17 or 11:10. He
> will then ask the congregation to join him in a kneeling,
> silent prayer. (*COF* 1996: 54)

The first minister stepped up to the table and began greeting the congregation. He seemed to be stalling, taking up several minutes without really saying anything, repeatedly looking towards the rear entrance. At last they came in. The back doors banged open and the boys noisily walked into the building in single file, their eyes on the floor. It was like a parade. Everyone, including the minister, stopped to watch as the line curved around into the back of the boys' section and turned into the pews.

The minister immediately launched into his sermon. "In the beginning, God created the heavens and the earth in six days, resting on the seventh day, the day that we call Saturday, the Sabbath." The preacher proceeded to tell the stories of Adam and Eve, the Forbidden Fruit, Cain and Abel, Noah and the Ark, and the Tower of Babel. He spoke in nearly constant monotone, with a lisp. He finished his sermon with a prayer. Everyone kneeled in silence for about two minutes, until he said "Amen."

> The second minister will continue to teach, by memory,
> from Genesis 12 to Exodus 15, lifting out types and figures pointing to Christ. (*COF* 1996: 54)

The second minister rose to the preacher's table. His sermon began after the Tower of Babel, progressing through the parting of the Red Sea by Moses. His sentences were also long and monotone, until the last word, the tone of which would be below the rest—his voice having slid down to the lower tone. Working together in this fashion, the two ministers summarized every major Old Testament story up to the Exodus, including the following: Abram and Sarah in Egypt, Abram and Lot Go Separate Ways, Abram becomes Abraham, Sodom Destroyed, Isaac Almost Sacrificed, Esau and Jacob,

Joseph and his Colorful Coat, Jacob Sends Sons to Buy Corn in Egypt, Moses Charged to Deliver the Jews from Bondage, and many more. The two sermons worked as a chronicle of the collective conscience. These are the stories that all members know. The second minister concluded his sermon by saying that "God has always worked through His people—as He continues to do."

The bishop rose along with the deacon. The two spoke briefly and the deacon was handed a copy of the Bible. The bishop sat back down and the Deacon approached the preacher's table. He greeted the congregation and proceeded with the following words: "The scripture that we were requested to read this morning is to be found in Paul's first letter to the Corinthians, 11, verses 23 to 29." Upon reading these verses to the congregation, he read two other passages from the New Testament, both about communion (as prescribed in the COF, Luke 22:1–23 and I Cor. 110:1–24). After encouraging the members to be attentive to the bishop's sermon, the deacon sat down.

> The bishop then speaks of Christ's last supper, His great suffering, His crucifixion, resurrection, and ascension, exhorting on both Scriptures the deacon has read. (COF 1996: 54)

The bishop formally greeted the church and proceeded to preach. Before saying anything about communion, he narrated the Passion Story, from the Last Supper up to the Resurrection. He then commented in detail on the selected passages read by the deacon. He stressed several key points of doctrine. Unlike Roman Catholics, who believe that communion involves consumption of the actual body and blood of Christ, Mennonites assert that the bread and wine are only symbols. The bishop argued as follows:

> Although we are not wise people, how could it be otherwise, since Jesus himself was the first to practice the ordinance? Are we to think that he was serving the

apostles parts of his body? Did he give them his blood to drink?

The bishop also discussed the meaning that communion should have for members of the church, along with who should partake of it. "As it is written, let each one examine themselves to find themselves worthy or not. It is for nobody else to know. . . . But, we do not offer this communion to those who come in off the street."

While the bishop continued to speak about the proper mindset for those about to partake of the Lord's Supper, the deacon and one of the ministers went to the side of the building, into the counsel room, returning with a basket of bread, wrapped in a white towel, and wine. About two liters of dark red wine were contained in a large oval glass bottle, about one fourth full. A heavy metal cup was also brought out and set down upon the table.

> Before each emblem is served, the bishop takes it in his hands and asks the congregation to arise. Whereupon he offers a short audible prayer of thanksgiving. "Oh Thou eternal, almighty God, we once more come before Thee to thank Thee for thine only begotten Son Jesus Christ, who came into this world and suffered His holy body to be broken for the remission of our sins. Wherefore we heartily say unto Thee, praise, honor, thanks, and eternal blessings, in the name of Jesus Christ our worthy Redeemer. Amen." (*COF* 1996: 55)

With his sermon finished, the bishop took a long and slender piece of white bread from the towel and held it in his outstretched left palm. "The congregation will stand." Everyone rose, even the children. Speaking very quickly, the bishop made the following announcement in a very serious tone of voice: "Anyone here that has anything to do with radios or CBs is not permitted to receive this communion." Immediately after this blunt announcement, the bishop bowed his head and gave thanks for the bread.

The bishop took a small part of the bread in his hand and ate it. As prescribed in the *COF*, he next proceeded to give a small bite-sized piece of bread to the first minister, then to the second minister, then to the deacon. The ministers immediately consumed the bread. The bishop next gave a bite to each of the seven songleaders, sitting at the Singers' Table. He then walked over to the oldest person sitting in the men's section, followed by the deacon carrying the basket of bread. There were about 50 men sitting on the men's side of the building. Distributing the bread took a long time. Nobody stirred or made a sound. Whenever one strip of bread was used up, the deacon gave the bishop another.

The bishop gave a bite of bread to the person across the aisle from me. Then, without even looking down at me, he reached over and gave the man on the other side of me his portion. A second later, the bishop was walking back down in the other direction.[2]

The bishop handed a piece of bread to every male member before crossing the building to the oldest female. As he walked slowly around the room, with the deacon following a few paces behind, he uttered various phrases. "Take, eat, for this is the body of the Lord Jesus." "This is the bread of life, it alone will satisfy the hunger of your soul." After the youngest female member had received her bread, he stopped in the middle of the building and asked if anyone had been passed over. "We would not want to forget anyone." Nobody was missed, so the bishop returned to the table and offered a prayer for the fruit of the vine. Members were told to kneel.

The bishop poured some wine into the heavy metal cup, took a sip, and passed it to the first minister, the second minister, the deacon, and so on. The same procedure was followed again, from the oldest and youngest male, down through the oldest and youngest female. The songleaders led five or six hymns during the distribution. Upon finishing, the bishop inquired, "Did we miss anyone?"

After Communion is served, the ministry testifies, and
the bishop leads in a kneeling audible prayer, after
which a hymn is sung. (*COF* 1996: 55)

Foot Washing

The first minister approached the preacher's table and spoke
briefly about the significance of the foot washing ordinance. "It is
important for the children to see us doing this with reverence, in
Christian love." While the minister spoke, three men and three
women brought in buckets of water and small stacks of folded
aprons made of towel cloth. The men and boys were given seven
buckets, positioned on the ground in front of the first pew of each
section.

The minister led a prayer, out loud, while the membership
kneeled. After the prayer, with one sweeping movement, the men
took off their black coats, revealing their white shirts. Throughout
the building, members removed their socks and shoes and neatly
placed them under the pews.

The minister will announce when all is ready, and all
members alternately wash each other's feet with water
(brother with brother and sister with sister), without
preference of person as to whose feet are being washed,
and dry them with the towel he or she is girded with.
(*COF* 1996: 56)

The bishop sat down on the front pew while the first minister
tied a long white apron around his waist. The minister knelt and
began to wash the other man's feet. He first wet his hands in the
water, then rubbed the bishop's toes, feet, and ankles. When he finished, the minister used his apron to dry the feet. Then the two
men traded places. After the bishop washed the first minister's feet,
the two shook hands and exchanged the kiss of brotherhood. With

his face close to the other man's, the minister paused to whisper several words into the bishop's ear.

> Then both shake hands with each other and give each other the kiss of peace, whereupon the one says: "The Lord will preserve and strengthen us in love"; the other says "Amen." (*COF* 1996: 56)

Following the example of the minister and bishop, the rest of the membership began the ceremony, using every available bucket of water. In pairs, members walked to one of the buckets of water. A member would sit on the pew and present his feet to be washed, then he would exchange places with his partner. After giving one another the kiss of peace, members exchanged whispers. The men kissed one another squarely on the lips, often creating a clearly audible smacking noise. The boys completed the ceremony faster than the older men, and their lackluster kisses were also aimed more at one another's cheek. The women seemed very gentle, taking more time than the men. During the ceremony, the songleaders led songs.

> While the washing of feet ceremony is being conducted, the rest of the congregation usually sings appropriate hymns. When all are finished and seated, a parting hymn will be sung and then the benediction is given. (*COF* 1996: 56)

When each pair finished the reciprocal act, they returned to their original seats. Back in their pews, the men put on their black jackets and all of the members put on their socks and shoes. The ordinance of foot washing was completed very quickly—in about 15 minutes. The biannual worship service was then concluded with a final prayer, led by the bishop.

Notes

1. *A Collection of Psalms and Hymns* 1977: 291.

2. Although I did not expect it, some members of the church antici-
pated that I would be offered communion. Indeed, other members thought
I had received it, despite the bishop's comment. After the service, a man
came up to me grinning and quietly said, "You didn't get no communion
did you?" He said that he did not understand why I was not included. "I
thought he'd give it to you. Maybe he didn't see you—you should have
spoke up." Still another Weaverlander told me: "The fact that you were not
served communion should not be a surprise to you since we do have a
closed communion, for members in good standing only. Following this
practice we do not need to pass judgment upon non-church members."

Chapter 6

The Discipline and Excommunication

Each thought and deed, His piercing eyes
  With strictest search survey;
The deepest shades no more disguise,
  Than the full blaze of day.[1]

The members of the Weaverland Conference of Old Order Mennonites live their lives in conformity with the "Church Discipline," or
the "Conference Report." The Discipline is an established system
of behavioral rules and plays a fundamental role in preserving the
integrity of the Weaverland community. These rules maintain the
difference between Old Order Mennonites and people in the world.
In this chapter, I discuss the Discipline of the Church from my perspective as a sociologist and explain how it regulates "appropriate"
ways for members to dress, talk, get from one place to another,
marry, earn money, entertain themselves, and relate to people of
the non-Mennonite world.

The members of every human group adhere to commonly
accepted social rules. As long as these rules are clearly defined,
individuals may communicate with one another and interact
meaningfully. This is the simple and powerful theme of the Old Testament story of the Tower of Babel. When the human builders of
the Tower became too proud of their construction, when they
began to think of themselves as gods, God took away their common
language and made it impossible for them to continue working.
When a society is not effectively organized by social rules, it
becomes "anomic" (Durkheim 1964). In a state of anomie, each
member of society follows his or her own behavioral standards and
individuals no longer know what behavior they may expect from
others. Perhaps Nietzsche was thinking of the Tower of Babel, or of
anomic society, when he claimed that "any custom is better than
no custom."

Old Order Mennonites seem to think of themselves as members of a distinctive community set apart from the rest of the
world. By conforming to the same behavioral rules, their difference
from the world is disclosed, made evident and plausible. At the
farmers' market, cattle auction, farm store, and bank, Mennonites
cannot avoid interaction with "people of the world." On such occasions, Old Order people rely on unique physical props and outward
behaviors to demonstrate their common identity and social dis-

tinction. For instance, black hats and white bonnets are signs that directly convey that Mennonites are "a different people." When Old Order Mennonites discuss or write about the things they are not, the things they do not believe in and will not allow themselves to do, they point at the people who live outside of their community. "*We* are not like *them*." By defining who and what they are not, the members of the church gain a collective understanding of what it means to be "Mennonite."

For individuals who share a communal identity, the ability to make meaningful distinctions between members and nonmembers creates the impression of a stable and ordered social environment:

> Societies attempt to achieve an orderly, coherent universe through the maintenance of a system of categories that organize perceptual data in terms of various classifications. . . . We would not even be able to think, let alone interact, if we could not identify the messages of our senses as establishing what something was like, what it was unlike, and how these things were related logically. (Crocker 1973: 69)

Weaverland Mennonites are members of a religious social system operating within a greater social environment. Like all social systems, the Mennonite congregation must work to retain its separate identity from the world (Dahm, Luhmann, and Stoodt 1972). This member/nonmember distinction is a human construction and is, at every moment, in danger of collapse. Indeed, it collapses every time a Mennonite chooses to leave the church or is expelled.

The fragile boundary between Mennonites and the world is effectively maintained by the behavioral rules of the church, articulated in the Discipline. Religious beliefs are not referenced in the Regulations of the Church—the code is completely action oriented. In their discussion of the word "discipline," the authors of *The Oxford English Dictionary* (1985) noted a thought provoking distinction:

"Etymologically, *discipline*, as pertaining to the disciple or scholar, is antithetical to *doctrine*, the property of the doctor or teacher; hence, in the history of the words, *doctrine* is more concerned with abstract theory, and *discipline* with practice or exercise." With or without shared religious beliefs (doctrine), the "discipie" can see his brethren by their actions. To be socially meaningful, the symbols that create the boundary around members of the church do not depend on what they might or might not signify.

The sociologist Kai T. Erikson (1966) described the way in which rules of behavior help preserve a social boundary around a society:

> A human community can be said to maintain boundaries, then, in the sense that its members tend to confine themselves to a particular radius of activity and to regard any conduct which drifts outside that radius as somehow inappropriate or immoral. Thus the group retains a kind of cultural integrity, a voluntary restriction on its own potential for expansion, beyond that which is strictly required for accommodation to the environment. Human behavior can vary over an enormous range, but each community draws a symbolic set of parentheses around a certain segment of that range and limits its own activities within that narrow zone. These parentheses, so to speak, are the community's boundaries. (p. 10)

With their Discipline, the Mennonites of the Weaverland Conference have drawn "a symbolic set of parentheses" around behaviors that are considered appropriate for members. The Weaverland community has socially constructed an internally meaningful code of conduct, a "self-referential system" that maintains authentic group membership (Luhmann 1985; 1997). By selecting one rule after another, their ability to communicate as a society has been established.

According to one of the ministers, the bishop is the only member of the Weaverland Mennonite community who actually has a written copy of the Regulations of the Church. Consequently, the membership only knows the Discipline from the bishop relating it to them. This takes place twice a year, just before the church celebrates communion. Because the Discipline is read only twice each year, members tend to have an imperfect recollection of precisely what it entails. Some members told me that the Conference Rules contained proscriptions that other members had never heard of. Hence, though the Discipline has been written down, members tend to incorrectly attribute items to and from it. A minister, for example, claimed that the Discipline did not specifically forbid members from visiting theaters, but did forbid them from buying lottery tickets. In fact, according to a knowledgeable member, both of these claims are incorrect.

Neither of these items is listed in the "Conference Report," as it is called. By the simple life style promoted in the "Conference Report" every one knows theaters and lotteries are off limits. Items like these sometimes appear in the collective counsels from all the churches. This Counsel Report follows the reading and explanation of the Conference Report. The rules of the Conference Report are binding where the Counsel Report is the counsel of the churches given as good advice concerning current issues. As one thinks back on the reading of the reports there may sometimes be a slight confusion on where the items actually did appear.

I asked a member to explain why the Conference and Counsel Reports were not published and distributed to the entire congregation. If this were done, members might be more likely to have a uniform understanding of the Rules of the Church. After consulting his bishop, this member relayed the following information:

The bishops are the only members of the Conference who have actual written copies of the Conference Rules. They do not publish the list of rules because they do make changes once in a while. They feel that if people had a printed copy of the rules, than they would be less likely to accept changes, if they had to be made.

The Weaverland Discipline is very similar to that of several other current Old Order Mennonite conferences, all based on the "Lancaster Conference *Ordnung*" created in 1881 (reprinted in Hoover 1982: 681–82). A minister reported that the Weaverland *Ordnung*, with very minor changes, is the same set of church regulations adopted by the Wisler Conference in 1931. The Wisler and Weaverlander Conferences continue to enjoy "full fellowship" with one another because they hold the same set of church regulations. This means that members may interact socially as if they were members of the same church.

The actual list of regulations in the Wisler *Ordnung* is comprised of 26 paragraphs. The first 11 paragraphs pertain to the proper organization of the church, selection of members, and the keeping of the ordinances. The rest of the regulations prohibit specified practices, such as those listed below (from the Wisler Conference Rules, in Hoover 1982: 909–10):

13. *Worldly Offices*: The brethren are not allowed to serve in any office except school director and road supervisor, and these are earnestly testified against.

15. *Matrimony*: We acknowledge a Christian matrimony between one man and one woman who are believers and lead a nonresistant life. If a member marries out of the church, that member shall be put back from council of brethren and communion until he acknowledges and openly confesses that he has transgressed the evangelical discipline of the church. . . .

16. *Pride:* . . . We earnestly testify against pride and haughtiness in every respect. Homes should be kept plain, funerals should be conducted in a plain and quiet way, also all that we possess, that we may be as lights in the midst of a crooked and perverse generation.

19. Lightning rods are forbidden and the insuring of buildings is testified against.

24. Attending theaters and other places of amusement is contrary to Bible teaching, hence it is forbidden.

Some of the most important practices commonly attributed to the Weaverland Discipline by members are not actually included in the official document. For example, the prescriptive norm requiring all members to drive only black cars was codified in written form in a pamphlet distributed to members in 1935. A 1945 reprint of the pamphlet includes the following two paragraphs (Hoover 1982: 698):

3. Conference having sanctioned the use of the automobile under certain restrictions as follows: The touring or phaeton. The roadster, if the rear seat is removed and not used. Closed cars that are out of style models. All cars in black color, no stripes, nor flashy trimmings.

4. Conference disapproves to make a display of folding tops.

The ministry of the church has since assembled a "very long" list of automobile makes and models that members are forbidden to own. Generally, members buy used cars that were manufactured in the United States. Vans, large touring sedans, and wagons are popular models in the community. When a car is purchased, members must paint the body and all chrome parts black and remove the radio. One member is usually asked to paint the cars and earns about $100 for his efforts. If a member drove a car deemed too flashy by the ministry, one with the wrong color, or if he failed to remove the radio, he would be expelled from the church, unless he repented of the transgression.

In addition to the moral fact regulating automobiles, the dress code for members is not actually a part of the official Discipline, but is nonetheless commonly attributed to it and compulsory. Around the home and in public settings, for example, women are required to wear coverings over their hair. This requirement is based on Paul's admonition to women in the New Testament: "But every woman that prayeth or prophesieth with her head uncovered dishonoureth her head; for that it is even as if she were shaven" (I Corinthians 11:5). Coverings can be bought through catalogs or constructed at home with purchased materials. The small bonnet is made of white netting and has narrow white or black ribbons that may or may not be tied underneath the wearer's chin. This covering is the only kind of covering that adult women in the church may wear. If a woman refused to wear it, she would be expelled. Similarly, male members must wear dark, collarless suits in church. A Weaverlander who wears a collar or a light-colored suit would certainly be considered a "disorderly" member.

When asked about why members follow the Discipline of the church, a member replied:

> The Discipline is something that we follow because it reminds us of the past, the old ways, they keep us together. . . . I like to feel like I'm helping others. Being a light to others. Doing good. I think the church does good. Following the regulations helps you do right, it helps you stay in the right.

This comforting sense of "staying in the right" by following the *Ordnung* is also evident in the following excerpt from a letter printed in an Old Order magazine:

I joined the church at seventeen and later found a decent, kind companion. Now when I read and hear of the wickedness of our times, how glad I am that I am in a group of people with a sturdy "Ordnung" to protect us against the Subtle One. (*Family Life* 1993: 3)

The church regulations codified in the Discipline are very difficult to change. As a result, the regulations provide members with a sense of stability and permanence. The appeal of "the older way" has kept members of the church from altering collective practices. According to one informant:

It is important to keep the traditions. Back when we wanted to change our seating arrangement in church, when we wanted to sit facing forward, most people supported the change. But others said that "our ancestors have been sitting towards each other in that there way for hundreds of years. We daren't change that." And you know, of course, that we didn't.

By their conformity to the Weaverland Church Discipline, members can be assured that they live within the authentic community of the saints. While it is never possible for a member to be completely certain of his or her salvation, one can know without a doubt whether or not one is conforming to the Regulations of the Church. If one does not live in conformity to the rules, one will be called to account by the community.

Expulsion: The Ultimate Communal Sanction

Members who transgress against the rules established in the "Gospel and the regulations of the church" and who do not repent of their sins are "expelled" from the Weaverland Church until they do so. Members believe that the Bible teaches them to separate themselves from "disorderly" people:

> If a member falls into gross sin or is not willing to be admonished in errors in his way of life, he shall be excommunicated from the church. When he shows repentance and amendment of life, and wishes to be reinstated again in the church, he will make his desire known by coming into the minister's room on a Sunday morning and presenting his application to the ministry, who then presents it to the congregation. The bishop will take counsel with the church concerning reinstating him. (*COF* 1996: 60)

The Weaverland manner of excommunication is not as complete as the "shunning" performed by the Old Order Amish. Regarding the Amish practice, Kephart and Zellner (1994) reported the following:

> The ultimate sanction is the imposition of the *Meidung*, also known as the "shunning" or "ban," but because of its severity, it is only used as a last resort. The followers of Jacob Amman have a strong religious orientation and a finely honed conscience—and the Amish community relies on this fact. . . . The ban is total. No one is permitted to associate with the errant party, including members of his or her own family. . . . Should any member of the community ignore the *Meidung*, that person would also be placed under the ban. (p. 27)

In contrast, "expelled" Weaverland Mennonites are permitted to attend worship services with their families and may even participate in the social activities of members. It is, nonetheless, strictly forbidden to allow expelled members to participate in the religious "ordinances" (foot washing, holy kiss, communion, counsel). It is not uncommon for officially excommunicated members to continue to attend church services.

If a member must be expelled, the bishop announces his or her name and the practice that is considered intolerable in front of the assembled congregation. From that moment on, it is hoped that the experience of expulsion will encourage the detached person to find his or her own way back into the realm of authentic membership. If the expelled person decides to mend his or her ways and rejoin the church, he or she must ask the bishop for the opportunity to ask forgiveness in front of the assembled congregation. I observed this ritual of reconciliation at the end of a normal Sunday worship service. Once the closing prayer was over, the bishop announced to the congregation that an expelled person, mentioned by name, desired to confess his sins and request membership in the church. He then exchanged glances with a man standing in the back of the men's section. Both men walked into the center of the building, in front of the entire congregation. The expelled man stood directly in front of the bishop with his hands clasped tightly at the waist and eyes cast to the floor. "Do you answer with yes that you have repented of your sin?" With a very brief look upward, the man whispered "yes." "Do you answer with yes that you have asked God to forgive you and that He has done so?" "Yes."

The bishop seemed to refrain from looking directly at the man, preferring instead to observe the congregation. Most of the members had their heads bowed. The bishop continued, "Because you have repented and been forgiven you are once again a member of the church. The rights of communion, foot washing, and counsel are restored to you."

The bishop then clasped the other man's hand and gave him the kiss of peace on the lips. After this ceremony, the two men sat down and the songleaders led two hymns about forgiveness and mercy.

The procedural rules dictating how the congregation must receive an expelled member who repents of breaking the Discipline are codified in the *Confession of Faith* (1996). It is essentially the same procedure that Bishop Jonas Martin followed nearly 100 years ago, after founding the Weaverland Conference (see "Martin's Personal Handbook," in Hoover 1982: 701–9).

After observing the church perform this ritual of reconciliation for the first time, I asked members after the service what the expelled man had done. I was startled by the variety of answers received. One member replied, "Oh, he was a drinker." Another reported, "Henry cheated on his wife." A third informant answered with, "That man went with women for money." Still another member simply replied that she did not remember what the man had done, "After all, he was expelled almost a year ago." Each time a member is expelled, the bishop is required to make the reason for expulsion completely clear, revealing the nature of the sin in front of everyone present. Even though he must do this, it seems evident that members do not feel it is important to specifically know what a "disorderly person" did. In fact, during the ritual of reconciliation, nobody seems to demonstrate much interest in the interaction between the bishop and the one repenting. Apparently, the important thing is that all members remain aware of the Regulations of the Church and conform to them, preserving the cultural integrity of the community.

While sanctions such as expulsion are actual practices that can be observed, the beliefs that uphold the statutes of the Discipline are not. The leadership of the church makes no concerted effort to instruct members as to why they should adhere to the church's rules. They do not attempt to monitor whether or not members of the church hold "correct and proper" Mennonite beliefs. Because they are externalized, the deviant acts of members are much easier to control than deviant thoughts. Their religious service does not include a recitation of the Apostle's Creed or any other confession of faith. For the Mennonites, maintaining correct and uniform behavioral discipline appears to be more important than maintaining correct and uniform religious doctrine.

The existence of a given norm in the Mennonite community is inherently tied to whether or not a sanction protects it. Sanctions encourage conformity to moral facts independently of a collective understanding or moral orientation. Mennonites learn *how* to follow the church Discipline and what happens to those who do not; but members are seldom taught *why* they ought to conform to the rules and what the reason behind each regulation is. It is generally taken for granted by members that each of the norms comprising the Discipline is legitimate and worth following.

Discussion: Moral Rules and Sanctions

Though many of a community's established rules can be broken without socially meaningful consequences, societies actively punish those members who do not conform to "moral rules." As Durkheim (1964) suggested, some social norms are considered important enough by the members of a group that transgression brings about an actual sanction. Such a norm may be called a "moral rule" or "moral fact." "Moral rules are invested with a special authority because they command. . . . Obligation is, then, one of the primary characteristics of the moral rule" (Durkheim 1953: 35–36). A Mennonite, for example, may be expelled from the church if he is discovered watching a movie in a theater. That members are not allowed to see films is a moral fact. In this case, loss of church membership is the specific sanction that enforces conformity. All of the members are aware of what will happen to their membership if they are found watching a movie, even if they personally do not believe that movies are evil.

Durkheim (1964) sharply distinguished general "rules of conduct" from what he called "moral facts":

> But how then shall we recognize the facts that are the
> object of this science, that is, the moral facts? . . . First
> of all, they clearly consist of rules of conduct; but even

so there are a number of facts of this kind which have
no moral character about them. For example, there are
the rules that a doctor must follow in the treatment of
this or that illness; others informing the manufacturer,
the merchant, the artist, the way to proceed to success.
(p. 424)

Warning his readers not to confuse such general rules of conduct with moral facts, Durkheim suggested two characteristics
peculiar to the latter: (1) society always intervenes to oppose devi-
ation from established moral facts, and (2) sanctions are applied to
those members of society who act counter to moral facts (1964:
424–25).

Sanctions provide feedback to individual actors, communi-
cating the socially constructed appropriateness or inappropriate-
ness of their behavior. The American sociologists Talcott Parsons
and Edward A. Shils (1951) proposed that there is a "polarity" of
social sanctions that includes rewards as well as punishments.

The culture is not only a set of symbols of communication but a *set of norms* for action. . . . The motivation of
ego and alter become integrated with the normative patterns through interaction. The polarity of gratification is
crucial here. An appropriate reaction on alter's part is a
gratifying one to ego. If ego conforms to the norm, this
gratification is in one aspect a reward for his conformity with it; the converse holds for the case of deprivation
and deviance. The reactions of alter to ego's conformity
with or deviance from the normative pattern thus
become sanctions to ego. (Pp. 106, 154)

This polarity of sanctions is well illustrated by the Weaverland Mennonites. If members of the church conform to the established moral facts of the community, they will be positively sanc-

tioned with the right to participate in communion, counsel, foot washing, organizational meetings, and leadership roles. If they do not conform, they will be the subject of gossip, stares, ridicule, or banishment. According to Robert Merton (1968), all human societies have two essential features in common: culturally defined goals that their members strive to achieve and acceptable modes of achieving them. In a manner similar to Durkheim, Merton maintained that societies tend to separate possible methods of goal attainment into categories of "acceptable" and "unacceptable" alternatives. Instead of using Durkheim's concept of the "moral fact," Merton used the term "regulatory norm" to refer to a patterned behavior that is deemed acceptable by society:

> Sociologists often speak of these controls as being "in the mores" or as operating through social institutions. Such elliptical statements are true enough, but they obscure the fact that culturally standardized practices are not all of a piece. They are subject to a wide gamut of control. They may represent definitely prescribed or preferential or permissive or proscribed patterns of behavior. In assessing the operation of social controls, these variations . . . must of course be taken into account. (p. 187)

Merton's analysis of regulatory norms is useful as it includes a positive and negative dimension that is lacking in Durkheim's concept of the moral fact. Indeed, a moral fact can require that a certain behavior be practiced *or* that it not be practiced. For instance, the Discipline proscribes the purchase of insurance and prescribes the pattern that a woman uses to make her cape dress. The Discipline also includes what Merton would identify as preferential norms. For example, "The brethren are not allowed to serve in any office *except* school director and road supervisor, *and these are earnestly testified against*" (emphasis added). The Conference also "testifies against" riding snowmobiles and three-wheel motorcycles.

Individual Mennonites can decide whether or not they will observe the preferential norms proscribing the use of musical instruments such as the piano and guitar. All members know that the leadership of the church "councils against using musical instruments." Nonetheless, some members elect to play instruments and others do not.

When norms are defined independently of sanctions, it is difficult to distinguish between *de facto* and *de jure* norms, or even between folkways and mores. Without sanctions to support them, norms can only be considered social conventions, patterns of behavior that are demonstrated by the members of a group. However, the normative order, what members *ought* to do, is not the same as what members *actually* do (Mizruchi and Perrucci 1973). *That is, a member can do what everybody else is doing, but it can be something that everybody knows that they ought not be doing.*

For example, Mennonites preach against the use of birth control. In the normative order, birth control is something that the community opposes. Nonetheless, the average family size of contemporary Mennonite families is shrinking. A member of the community attempted to explain this inconsistency between the normative and factual orders with the statement: "We may not *believe* in using [birth control], but that doesn't mean we don't use it." When it comes to traditional community values, Mennonites esteem large patriarchal families. However, regulating family size has economic benefits that the entire community enjoys. Hence, while the ministers preach against birth control in church, husbands and wives use it to keep the size of their families under control. "The ministers know that we use it [contraceptives] and they know who passes it out. But, they let on as if they did not know."

While the Regulations of the Church do limit the personal freedom of members, the regulatory system is a product of the entire community and, hence, commonly accepted as legitimate. As explained in chapter 5, the ministers of the Weaverland Conference, which includes all local bishops, preachers, and deacons, formally "hold conference" twice a year to discuss the state of the church. Any member of the church may charge one of the ministers, as his representative, to bring an issue or problem to the attention of the assembled ministers. Sometimes members will suggest that the Regulations of the Church be changed, that, for instance, a certain rule be taken away or added to the list. When they "hold conference," the ministers will debate the matter, come to a decision through consensus, and report back to the local congregations. Because the Discipline is produced in this democratic manner, each member of the community can see his or her own hand in maintaining the regulatory system. In the next chapter, I explain how the specific rules of the Discipline may be further legitimated—in the unlikely event that they are ever questioned.

Note

1. *A Collection of Psalms and Hymns* 1977: 175.

Chapter 7

Church Rules and Their Legitimation

Thy flesh, perhaps thy chiefest care,
Shall crawling worms consume;
But ah! destruction stops not there—
Sin kills beyond the tomb.[1]

In a study focusing on comparatively more modern and liberal Mennonites, Redekop, Ainlay, and Siemens (1995) investigated how Mennonite businessmen rationalize their participation in the "capitalist world economy." To deal with any moral problems that might surface as they conduct their business in the world, Mennonite entrepreneurs develop a coping strategy that Redekop and his associates called "compartmentalization." "Rather than integrating faith and business, they have opted for a compartmentalization of life to maintain ideological purity while engaging in economic practices that sometimes seem at odds with the Anabaptist-Mennonite ethos" (Redekop, Ainlay, and Siemens 1995: 240). Compartmentalization helps entrepreneurial Mennonites maintain a righteous self-image even though they occasionally engage in practices that they believe are unethical. If they could not compartmentalize their faith and practice, Mennonites would have trouble rationalizing their actions as capitalists.

According to Redekop, Ainlay, and Siemens, Mennonites have "developed a compulsion to rationalize (especially in moral terms) all actions to the tiniest detail and to engage in actions that will be defensible when the inevitable (and final) interrogation occurs" (1995: 177). In my observation of Old Order Mennonites, however, I find that members demonstrate little concern for rationalizing their actions. As long as everyone abides by the Regulations of the Church, nobody will be called to explain their actions. It seems that justifications first become necessary when the Discipline of the church is weakened and members begin to lead diverse lifestyles. In his study of schisms among the Mennonites, Kniss (1996: 19) reports that the Mennonite Church's Lancaster Conference *added* explanations and justifications for each of it rules even while relaxing its Discipline and becoming more like the world.

Unless they would risk expulsion, members of the Weaverland Church must conform to the many moral rules of their community. If, as an illustration, a member drove to church one Sunday morning in a white vehicle, he would certainly attract criticism from his peers. The disorderly member would be told that unless the car is painted black he should drive away and never come back.

In traditional communities such as the Old Order Mennonites, "one may not, without calling into effect negative social sanctions, challenge as valueless what has come to be traditional in that society" (Redfield 1947: 303). Regarding conduct in homogenous folk societies, the anthropologist Robert Redfield maintained (1947):

> Behavior in the folk society is traditional, spontaneous, and uncritical, what one man does is much the same as what another man does, and the patterns of conduct are clear and remain constant throughout the generations. . . . The congruence of all parts of conventional behavior and social institutions with each other contributes to the sense of rightness that the member of the folk society feels to inhere in his traditional ways of action. (p. 303)

Most of the time, established customs and moral facts are simply *taken for granted* by members of the Weaverland community and followed without much thought or discussion. Every Mennonite *knows* that his car must be painted black. All know this without having a common understanding about *why* it must be painted black. Redfield (1947: 303) maintained "the value of every traditional act or object or institution is, thus, something that the members of the society are not disposed to call into question, the doing so is resented."

Whether or not members resent it, a moral fact may spontaneously become the object of controversy and debate. Returning to the illustration above, let us suppose the owner of the white car demanded to be told exactly why it was so important for all members of the church to paint their cars black. He might protest, "Why is a white car less righteous than a black one?" In response to this challenge, the established moral fact would have to be defended against alternative ways of doing things—its specific *rationale* would need to be put into words (Scott and Lyman 1973; Lyman and Scott 1989: 184). Sociologists Marvin Scott and Stanford Lyman have described how "accounts," such as excuses and justifications, are demanded of *individuals* who break social norms:

> An account is a linguistic device employed whenever an action is subjected to valuative inquiry. Such devices are a crucial element in the social order since they prevent conflicts from arising by verbally bridging the gap between action and expectation. Moreover, accounts are "situated" according to the statuses of the interactants, and are standardized within cultures so that certain accounts are terminologically stabilized and routinely expected when activity falls outside of the domain of expectations. (1987: 47)

In their analysis of accounts, Lyman and Scott did not attempt to describe what happens when an individual member demands that his *community* account for its norms. When this occurs, the fragile nature of the moral order is often revealed. This is the focus of my analysis in the present chapter.

There are many different ways that a man can wear his beard. Yet, consider the following excerpt from an Amish reader's letter to the editor of a Mennonite periodical:

> I, too, can see the danger of losing the beard in our churches and I am thankful to God for giving me stronger convictions on the beard than I had at one time. Since then I notice it more when I see someone with his bare chin sticking out in front of a neck beard, or with his beard trimmed short. (*Family Life* 1983: 4)

Amish men conform to the moral fact of wearing full beards without mustaches. Why do they shave underneath their noses? Because—and here is the legitimating account—"mustaches are worn by military men, we do not believe in violence." In contrast, the men of Old Order Mennonite churches follow a moral fact that proscribes any facial hair. For both Amish and Mennonite men, there is only one "correct" way in which to wear a beard. The accepted moral fact is evident for each congregation and may, if required, be supported by legitimating accounts. While it is perhaps easy for a nonmember to imagine Mennonites growing beards and the Amish shaving, members are compelled to conform to their group's current standards, their collective "public definition of being" (Mannheim 1982: 334).

Levels of Legitimation Accounts

When discussions about the legitimacy of a moral fact arise, members of a society provide each other with reasons why particular ways of doing things are the "best" and the "only" way things should be done. Such discourse primarily involves the exchange of relatively rational accounts that "prove" the necessity of accepted moral facts, explaining why they are necessary and good in a convincing manner. If a custom is to be respected, it cannot be viewed as a meaningless contingency—something that may just as well be done differently.

Building upon the German sociologist Karl Mannheim's work, Peter Berger and Thomas Luckmann (1966: 87–90) suggested that discourse about moral facts occurs on various epistemological levels. The levels are distinguished according to their theoretical complexity. The most fundamental level of knowledge is common sense, while progressively more complex levels include aphorisms, specialized rhetoric, and metaphysical rhetoric. For those areas of social life that are common to all members of the community, legitimation accounts, if they are required at all, are taken from the arsenal of "common sense." When a moral fact is maintained by common sense, its legitimacy is maintained in a timeless, impersonal, and matter-of-fact manner. For example, a child that wishes to stay home from school will be told quite simply that "all children must go to school."

Nothing more than unadorned common sense stands behind legitimation accounts such as "that is just the way we do it," "that is the way it is," "everyone knows that it must be so." Nonetheless, the normative order of every society is predominantly supported by these "pretheoretical" common sense pronouncements (Berger and Luckmann 1966: 87). Mannheim described this elementary manner of legitimation as follows:

> The "It" inside us observes and regulates the world. "It is so," the proverbs maintain with thundering certainty (at least that is the spirit in which they speak to us); unquestionable and undialectical pronouncements of life experience. "That is the way it must be," announce the proverbial declarations and living laws that are sanctioned by folkways and tradition. (1982: 337)

My inquiries about the significance of Mennonite behavior were most frequently answered by members with the reply, "that's just the way we Mennonites do it." Legitimation accounts based in common sense work well until children (and adults) begin to critically question "what everybody knows." This does not happen often because people, in the course of their everyday lives, generally have other things to think about. The overwhelming authority of common sense primarily lies in the inability of individuals to make every decision on their own, carefully contemplating the reasonable alternatives in every course of action.

Underneath common sense pronouncements lies a more complex level of knowledge from which legitimation accounts can be drawn. When "that's the way everybody does it" fails to be convincing, moral facts may be legitimated by the citation of a witty aphorism, a proverb, folk wisdom, or some other collectively owned account. After a boy refuses to get up at a reasonable hour "just because that is what a good boy must do," a father might try using the well-known phrase "Early to bed, early to rise, makes a man healthy, wealthy, and wise." If that fails to get Junior out of bed, the father might recall the well-known account, "Spare the rod, spoil the child." Even if he must physically force his stubborn son out of bed, the old phrase will help him feel comfortable doing so. Indeed, when I asked why Mennonites spank their children, a grandfather asked if I had not heard what happens if the rod is spared.

When the common stock of knowledge is insufficient to resolve questions about the public definition of being, it may be because the society has evolved into a state of higher differentiation. When members begin to do different things in their daily lives, the public definition of being becomes fragmented into specialized discourses, each with its own corresponding manners of legitimation. According to Mannheim (1982) and Berger and Luckmann (1966), legitimation accounts that employ an axiom connected to a specific discourse or practical situation are grounded in a third level of knowledge.

In a complex modern society, component organizations will construct their own norms and values, supported by their own accounts. A businessman can justify his competitive behavior by situating it within the discourse of free enterprise. In capitalist discourse, greed and ambition combine to turn "private vice into public virtue." However, a doctor who provides care only to patients who can afford to pay her cannot justify her actions within the discourse traditionally used by her professional peers. The Hippocratic Oath specifically requires physicians to treat anyone who requires attention. Educators, civil servants, politicians, farmers, and the members of other functionally differentiated subgroups possess norms and values peculiar to their specific subgroup. Consequently, an action that is considered legitimate for one group may be considered illegitimate by another.

The extent of a social group's internal diversity influences the kinds of accounts used to legitimate moral facts (Mannheim 1982). When the members of a group lead different life-styles, normative discourse tends to increase in abstraction, leaving the realm of universal practice. Instead of appealing to a uniform tradition or the common sense of all members to justify moral rules, heterogeneous groups tend to "diversify" their collective conscience into specialized branches with relative autonomy. Thus, such societies replace a monolithic discourse of legitimation, assuming one has developed beyond the level of common sense, with one that is compartmentalized and functionally specific (Luhmann 1991; 1994; 1997). Whatever norms remain on the universal level are typically of a superficial nature, as they must be shared by diverse subgroups who have relatively little in common.

On the fourth and deepest level of knowledge, a legitimation account may be taken from an all-encompassing, metaphysical discourse, invoking cosmic significance to all aspects of everyday and specialized life. The Weaverland Church Discipline, for example, affects virtually all aspects of life: what kind of food members should eat, what kind of clothing they should wear, how much they should work, how they should be entertained, and how they should worship. Such discourse imposes a metaphysical order upon the world, a "sacred canopy" (Berger 1990) that encompasses all partial discourses. Moral rules concerning things as diverse as black cars, white bonnets, lightning rods, lottery tickets, school dances, working on Sunday, adultery, drinking, and shaving legs may all be legitimated by reference to an overarching system of religious knowledge. The color of a car becomes sacred if it determines whether or not a member may receive the Holy Communion, which in turn determines whether or not a soul may enter the gates of heaven.

One Sunday after church I spoke with three Mennonite men about science and religion. An interesting controversy arose and was immediately resolved when a member employed a fourth-level legitimation account, which categorically brought scientific knowledge under the sacred canopy of religious knowledge. A partial transcript of the conversation follows.

MEMBER A: How can the Mormons believe that Jesus came to America after the crucifixion?

MEMBER B: I understand they think that some Jews came over on a boat, like Noah's ark. Jesus came to see them. Is that right? Where did they get an idea like that. . . . We don't believe that.

AUTHOR: Well, I have heard that their church spends money for archeological research in North and South America. If they found influences of Jewish culture on this continent, it would support their beliefs.

MEMBER B: Sure. People try to use science to prove everything. The "missing link" is something, you know. They build up some creature from a bone or two and want to prove evolution.

MEMBER A: Aren't they trying to find out what happened to the dinosaurs? Didn't they find scientific evidence of a great flood?

AUTHOR: I think I remember hearing something about the flood destroying the dinosaurs. What do you think about that theory?

MEMBERS A and B: That sounds good. Makes sense. (General agreement)

MEMBER C: (After a pause) No. Nope. That can't be what happened to them. We know that can't be true.

MEMBER A: How do we know that?

MEMBER C: Because we know that God told Noah to take two of every kind in the ark. So he must have taken the dinosaurs, if there were any.

MEMBERS A, B, and AUTHOR: (Express agreement with nods)

MEMBER B: You know what I wish? I wish that Noah had slapped that pair of mosquitoes when he had the chance.

Norms, Power, and Legitimate Authority

In his sociological analysis of political authority types, Max Weber suggested that a powerful person (or government) does not only attempt to maintain power through physical force, economic incentives, or intellectual justifications. Rather, an authority figure seeks to instill and preserve among his subjects the *belief* that his power is legitimate (1972: 122). If citizens believe that their government's laws are just, they will abide by them without police enforcement. Weber outlined three different justifications that are typically called upon to maintain the belief that a given political authority is legitimate. Authority may be accepted as legitimate because it is thought to be traditional, legal-rational, or charismatic.

Weber's three ideal types of legitimate authority have been frequently used to clarify sources of political power, but they may also help explain why individuals normally conform to the moral rules of their social group. The established norms of every social group are believed to be legitimate by its members. In support of the validity and integrity of their common moral rules, members of groups construct ideological justifications that provide rationales for their necessity, as described in the previous discussion.

On Sunday mornings, "because it has always been done so," Old Order Mennonites park their black automobiles in a circle surrounding the church building. The men let the women and girls out at the Women's Door, drive around to an available parking space, and back their vehicle into place. After turning off the ignition, they sit still for several minutes in their seats before getting out and entering the building through the Men's Door.

I asked members why they always back into their parking positions. The two most frequent replies were, "I never thought about it," and "That's the way we've always done it." Employing one of Weber's terms, these members are legitimating their shared practice with the authority of "tradition." One older member thought about it for several minutes before recalling that before the church adopted automobiles, their buggies were always backed into their parking places, with the horses all facing the same direction, toward the church. The men stayed with the animals for a few minutes to look after them. This member concluded, "I guess we just carried over the old way of parking the buggies." In this situation, all of the members know the "correct" way to park their automobiles. If anyone ever parked without backing up to face the church, they would be violating a clearly established norm. The parking norm is still practiced despite the fact that most members do not know the history of it. According to the sociologist Robert Merton, it is not uncommon for "activities originally conceived as instrumental [to be] transmuted into self-contained practices, lacking further objectives. The original purposes are forgotten and close adherence to institutionally prescribed conduct becomes a matter of ritual" (1968: 188).

In the late 1800s, members of the Old Order Mennonite community began a heated debate over the cultivation and use of tobacco, a controversy that is still unresolved. Both sides attempt to justify their positions with legitimating accounts. "Progressive" members argue that tobacco use is sinful and unhealthy, that the farmers who raise it contribute to a worldly life-style. This line of reasoning is echoed in the following two letters to the editor of an Old Order periodical:

> Sometimes we see some very disgusting situations. Like the bishop who preaches an inspiring wedding sermon, then lights up ten minutes after the last song is sung. Or the visiting minister who preaches about self-denial, and crucifying our fleshly desires, and then just as he is leaving, he lights up a big cigar. In the Bible we read: Everything you do with words or deeds, do it all in the name

of the Lord and thank God and the Father. Would it be
possible to smoke or chew in the name of the Lord, or
would we ever stop and thank God for a cigar? (*Family
Life* 1984c: 14–15)

"Who am I to call unclean anything that God has created and called clean?" Suppose your son or the next generation comes and says, "If God caused the marijuana
plant and the poppy plant to grow and called it clean,
why can't we use it, if we use it moderately?". . . If
tobacco would be forbidden here in our churches, it is
not so likely that these stronger drugs would be posing a
threat to us today.[2] (*Family Life* 1984c: 15)

The authors of these two letters strongly desire that the
church institute a proscriptive moral rule against using tobacco.
The accounts used to legitimate the rule correspond to the three
Weberian types sketched above. In a legal-rational mode, it is
argued that tobacco should be prohibited because it will lead down
a slippery slope to illegal drugs, it threatens the community, and it
involves health risks. Appealing to a traditional authority, a Bible
verse is cited. It is also suggested that the personal authority, the
charisma, of spiritual leaders would be compromised by their
tobacco smoke.

Mennonites who favor the use and cultivation of tobacco currently argue that God would not have created it had He not
approved of it, that tobacco has important medicinal uses, and that
it can be safely enjoyed as a blessing when used in moderation.
Supporting scripture is likewise called into play:

And so, my brother, if I use tobacco or do not use it, if I
farm tobacco or do not farm it, if I drink wine or do not
drink it, I hope to remain as the Apostle Paul recommended in his letter to the Romans in the fourteenth

chapter, the third verse, "Let not him that eateth despise him that eateth not, and let not him that eateth not judge him that eateth." *(Family Life* 1984b: 4)

Once again, the accounts used to legitimate the use of tobacco are diverse, corresponding to the three different Weberian types. An Old Order Mennonite who occasionally used tobacco explained to me that the practice was acceptable, because "Even Bishop Martin favored tobacco." As I related in chapter 2, Jonas Martin was the Mennonite leader who organized the "conservative" wing in the church schism of 1893, out of which the Weaverland Conference emerged. Grounding a contested norm with a charismatic account, if the respected bishop approved of tobacco, then it must be legitimate. Interestingly, Martin legitimated the cultivation of tobacco with a calculated legal-rational account. Defending its use against the "progressives" who desired to prohibit it, Martin proclaimed, *"Von ma de Tabak abschneit kommt die Hochmut in de gmeh"* (If we cut out tobacco, pride will come into the congregation) (see Hoover 1982: 509). The labor-intensive methods required for tobacco cultivation kept the men and boys busy working and was also the most lucrative crop to farm. If another crop were planted, many men would probably need to work in "public shops" with worldly people in order make ends meet. Perhaps Bishop Martin legitimated the permissive norm regarding tobacco with the account, "Idle hands are the devil's workshop." He may have also condoned the practice in order to preserve the financial independence of members from the surrounding world.

Communicated from one member of society to another, legitimating accounts persuade members to conform voluntarily to moral rules. If these accounts fail, there is always excommunication. As Durkheim noted, "the reality of an obligation is certain only if it is manifested by some sanction" (Durkheim 1964: 426). Repressive instruments, such as expulsion, are required when members no longer act as though they believe in the legitimacy of established moral facts (Sanderson 1991: 276). When a community fails to repress members who transgress against the traditional moral order, it is likely that the community is experiencing anomie, a state in which the normative order has become uncertain and members no longer agree on what constitutes legitimate behavior (Mizruchi and Perrucci 1973).

I find that Weaverland Mennonites tend to create legitimation accounts spontaneously, whenever they are needed. They do not seem to reflect upon "the official Mennonite worldview" and how it might justify certain practices, nor do they consult their copy of the *Confession of Faith* booklet or the Bible. Different members typically provide different accounts to legitimate the same moral fact. Indeed, it is not uncommon for members to disagree about the "real" reason for a certain moral rule, even while agreeing that it is a necessary practice. Apparently, the members of this community learn *how* to conform to group norms, without learning *why* each practice has been determined necessary or legitimate.

Members of the Weaverland Conference in New York State seem unable, in any systematic manner, to legitimate or account for their moral rules. To have this ability, members would need to share an orthodox ideology—a vocabulary of justifications that explain why the group's rules are necessary and make "good sense." I believe such an ideology has not yet developed beyond traditional "common sense" because these Mennonites have not previously been exposed to people who would question their lifestyle. They have not decided to go out into the world and propagate a certain gospel. Instead, along with other Old Order groups, the Weaverlanders have generally attempted to stay away from people who live differently than they do. The Weaverland settlement in New York State is, in this respect, a significant move in a new direction. This is the subject of the next chapter.

Notes

1. *A Collection of Psalms and Hymns* 1977: 336.

2. The writer of this letter acknowledges that Old Order communities were struggling with the problem of drug abuse as early as 1984. In more recent years, this problem has attracted widespread publicity. Two specific cases are worth mentioning here. In 1993, an Old Order Mennonite farmer in Mexico was caught growing marijuana amidst his corn. According to drug enforcement agents, Mennonites are responsible for approximately 20 percent of the illegal drugs smuggled into Canada. Between 1989 and 1995, United States and Canadian customs officials made more than 30 drug seizures involving Mennonites (*Dallas Morning News* 1995). From an interview with a U.S. customs official in El Paso, Texas, I learned that border guards never bothered to search Old Order Mennonites: "The group's reputation and old-fashioned appearance led us to believe that they were beyond suspicion. It took a dog to sniff out the first truck load of pot." In 1998, a federal court in Philadelphia indicted two Amish men for selling cocaine and metamphetamine. Over the course of five years, the two men allegedly received drugs from members of a notorious motorcycle gang and distributed them at Amish youth gatherings (*Los Angeles Times* June 25, 1998). These unfortunate cases of drug trafficking by members of Old Order communities support the thesis of this book. A member may dress the part and follow all of the behavioral rules of the church—regularly participating in religious rituals—and still believe that smuggling drugs is acceptable.

Chapter 8

The Attraction of
Another Church

O Happy day when saints shall meet
To part no more, the thought is sweet;
No more to feel the rending smart
Oft felt below, when Christians part.[1]

Individuals seem predisposed to accept the legitimacy of their own group's way of life. It is, of course, comforting to believe that inherited ways of living are the "best" ways to live. "Ethnic groups are inherently ethnocentric, regarding their own cultural traits as natural, correct, and superior to those of other groups, who are perceived as odd, amusing, inferior, or immoral" (Yetman 1991). However, when one is exposed to new ways of doing things, to different social institutions, the legitimacy of one's own way of life can be "put into question" (Plessner 1964: 48). When members of a group become aware of the idiosyncratic and contingent nature of their beliefs and norms—when they realize that other communities observe different customs and worship other gods but still appear to function well—a legitimation crisis may occur (Berger and Luckmann 1966). For, if other people can live without conforming to the social facts that I have been taught to accept, what compels me to abide by the normative standards of my community?

In this chapter I discuss the relationship between Weaverland Old Order Mennonites and Eastern Mennonites, another group of conservative Mennonites who recently settled in New York State. While the Weaverlanders are not evangelistic and rarely discuss religious practices and beliefs in any formal manner, the Eastern Mennonites actively defend the "singular" legitimacy of their own behavioral norms and religious dogma. The evangelistic character of Eastern Mennonites is an attractive quality for some Weaverlanders. Within a period of a few years, at least 15 Weaverland families have left their community to join the Eastern Mennonites.

If they decide to join the Eastern Mennonite Church, Weaverland Mennonites do not have to change much about the way they live. Members of the two churches share the same Mennonite-Anabaptist heritage. They are both conservative churches that value separation from the world and enforce similar behavioral regulations.[2] Both congregations celebrate the same religious rituals and, when it comes to fundamentals, they profess the same theology. Nonetheless, the two churches are different enough that one is losing members to the other. How might the attraction of the Eastern Mennonites be explained from a sociological perspective?

I believe that the Weaverland Mennonite Church is losing members to the Eastern Mennonite Church because it does not prepare its members to give ideological justifications or accounts (Scott and Lyman 1973) for group practices and beliefs. This was not a problem for members of the congregation in the past, when they lived closely together in "Pennsylvania Dutch Country," among neighbors who took their life-style for granted. According to John Hostetler, an observer of the Amish,

> Many sectarian societies, including the Amish, make little or no attempt to communicate their message. They recognize instinctively that authentic communication would mean greater literacy, education, and sophistication, and this would mean the beginning of the end. . . . A way of living is more important than communicating it in words. The ultimate message is the life. An Amish person will have no doubt about his basic convictions, his view of the meaning and purpose of life, but he cannot explain it except through the conduct of his life. (1993: 8)

Hostetler's comments well describe the traditional disposition of most Old Order Mennonites. However, the migration to New York State has brought about two dramatic changes in the social life of Weaverland Mennonites—resulting in a "deficit" of religious knowledge.

For Weaverland Mennonites, the migration to New York effectively decreased the frequency of social interaction among members, their social density (Durkheim 1964), while it increased the frequency of interaction with nonmembers. Under these altered circumstances, it appears that some Weaverland Mennonites have an increased need for religious knowledge—intellectual accounts to explain their traditional norms and values.

Compared with their peers who remained in Pennsylvania, Weaverland Mennonites who migrated to upstate New York have more frequent interaction with people outside of the church who do not understand or accept Old Order institutions. Consequently, members must come to terms with the contingent nature of their moral facts: things can be done differently. When a Mennonite sees his neighbor out working the Sunday before a snowstorm, it may be difficult for him to appreciate having to keep the Sabbath. And when his neighbor asks him why he cannot touch money on Sunday, why he paints a perfectly good white car black, why he does not watch television, why his girls always wear long dresses, and how come his wife wears the unusual hat, he may feel pressured to provide meaningful explanations.

Unlike the Weaverland community, the Eastern community teaches its members how to account for their unique institutions. The leaders of the Eastern Mennonite Church increase the self-confidence of members by teaching them in Sunday school how to provide reasons for the rules they follow, encouraging them to interact as missionaries with people of the world, and claiming to have a more "progressive spirituality." Most importantly, the ministry of this church makes a coordinated effort to produce orthodoxis of belief among its membership. In this sense, having evolved from a reliance on rituals to a reliance on beliefs in maintaining social solidarity, it is a more modern group. As Gluckman asserted (1962: 42–43), human societies progress from demonstrating "specific and traditional ritual, to generalized universalistic belief."

Comparing the Two Congregations

The Church Buildings

There is no "Visitors Welcome" sign out in front of the Weaverland church building. In fact, there is not even a sign identifying it as a church building. During nearly three years of regular attendance, I never saw a visitor enter the church, with the exception of the friends and family of members, who frequently come up from Pennsylvania. This Weaverland Mennonite Church makes no effort to attract new members from the world. The size of the church is predominantly maintained by inducting the children of members. To a lesser extent, the church also attracts members of more conservative Old Order conferences, such as the Groffdale Mennonites or Amish, who may desire a slightly more permissive Discipline.

The most significant force keeping members in the Weaverland community is probably the reluctance to break with tradition. In answer to my question of why he belongs to the church, one member told me: "I was raised in the church, belonging to it was never a question." This reply, in different combinations of words, was repeated over and over by members of the community. Evidently, most Weaverlanders are members of their church by default, persuaded to join only by a reluctance not to join.

In criticism of Mennonites who accept membership in the church because of family tradition, an Old Order minister told me the following:

> You know most of us were all born and raised in the church. We can count back the many generations to our forefathers who originally came over to Lancaster. We have original Mennonite family names like Martin, Zimmerman, and Burkholder. But you know we each and every one of us must decide on our own to join the church of Christ.
>
> A line back to the forefathers will not make you a member of the church. An old Mennonite name will not make a Christian out of you. At some time in each person's life a personal decision must be made to come out of the world, become a Mennonite, and start living like one.

This minister believed that people should make a conscious decision to join the church only after an introspective evaluation of alternatives. In reality, however, it seems that most Weaverland Mennonites join the church along with their peers once they turn 14 years of age. This is socially expected and a 16-year-old who has still not become a member would certainly be stigmatized.

The Eastern Mennonite Church building is situated just a few miles away from the Weaverland Mennonite Church. So that visitors do not miss their turn, members have placed a large sign on the corner of the intersection. The sign says "Eastern Mennonite Church of Waterloo; Sunday School 9:00; Worship Service 10:00; Everyone Welcome." A black arrow on the sign points down the road.

Entering the main doors of the Eastern Mennonite Church, one comes into a large foyer. There is a coat and hat rack for men on the right of the foyer, with a rack for women's coats and outer bonnets on the left. There is a small shelf holding religious tracts on the left wall of the room. Two bathrooms are positioned along the right wall of the foyer, and a nursery for babies is on the left wall.

In the Weaverland church, women and men have separate entry rooms, coats and hats are hung on individual hooks on the walls, and there is no collection of religious tracts. The bathrooms at the two churches are very different. At the Eastern church, the men's bathroom is a large room with tile floor and painted walls. There are two ceramic urinals, two toilet stalls, two sinks with several bars of soap and paper towels, and a large mirror. At the Weaverland church, the bathroom is outside the main building in a shed, built on top of a concrete slab. There is a single toilet stall, one sink, and a long stainless steel trough urinal with a faucet flush. There is no large mirror, soap, or towels. The Weaverland bathroom is rather dark and smells like a lavatory, whereas the bathroom at the other church is perfumed and brightly lit with florescent tubes.

From the foyer of the Eastern church, one enters the main auditorium through two sets of double doors, both of which are propped open and attended by ushers. One of the ushers greets each person at the door of the auditorium and accompanies him or her to the first possible vacant seat from the front of the main hall on the appropriate side—men on the right and women on the left. As do the Weaverlanders, the Eastern Mennonites segregate the sexes. However, instead of having them sit at distant extremes of a rectangular building, they divide the rectangle in half long ways, so that only a narrow aisle divides the sexes. Consequently, a male sitting in the back pew may actually be closer to a female, sitting across the aisle on his left, than to the next male, sitting several rows in front. In the Weaverland church, the women sit across the room from the men, with the Singer's Table placed long ways between them. While the Eastern Mennonites all face forward in their pews looking toward the pulpit, the Weaverland men and women face each other, with the "preacher's table" off to the side of the auditorium. All of the Eastern Mennonites sit facing the preacher; but only the young people face forward at the Weaverland church.

The main auditorium at the Eastern church is about 25 meters long. There are 25 wooden pews, 12 for women and 12 for men, with one pew set behind the pulpit, facing the congregation. The pews have maple seats and sides, with oak backs. Compared with the furniture in the Weaverland church, the woodwork is of poor quality. At the front of the auditorium, a wooden pulpit stands upon a raised platform about 10 inches above the floor. When one of the ministers preaches from the pulpit, a microphone amplifies his voice and two spotlights shine down on him from the ceiling. There is no elevated pulpit, spotlight, or microphone in the Weaverland church building.[3]

The interior walls of the Eastern church are painted pastel green, the ceiling is white, and the floor is covered with a short brown carpet. Four large electric ventilation fans hang from the ceiling. There are four double-hung windows along the right wall, two at the front, three on the left, with the missing window replaced by an emergency exit. Sitting in one of the pews, one can see a scenic wooded area outside of the left front window and a quaint dairy farm on top of a hill on the right.

Instead of electric fans, the Weaverland building has six square passive ventilation holes in the ceiling that are opened by pulling on strings from a central location. Windows are positioned symmetrically in the building and are placed too high for members to see anything from their pews but the topmost leaves on the maple trees that grow in the parking lot. While the nine windows in the Eastern church building have paper shades that can be rolled down to shut out direct light, the shades in the Weaverland church are too wide to fit into their frames, but do not cover the entire window when unrolled.[4] The Weaverland building is illuminated by naked light bulbs attached to the ceiling. Covered lights are found inside the Eastern church.

Sunday School

To begin services at the Eastern church, one of the ministers greets the congregation and leads an opening prayer. Then he announces that the children may go to their appropriate Sunday school classes. Children are dismissed in an orderly and disciplined fashion, according to their age category (first preschool, then the primary grades, older grades, young people). The Weaverland Mennonites are opposed to Sunday School, considering it a "worldly institution started by the Baptists and Methodists."

After the children and young adults are dismissed for their Sunday school classes, the bishop requests that the remaining adults move closer to the front of the building. In preparation for their lesson, members are expected to have studied a chapter from a booklet entitled *Adult Bible Studies*. The teacher normally begins the lesson by reading a few paragraphs from his special edition of the booklet, and then asks a few questions of his students.

One of the Sunday School sessions that I observed in the Adult Class was on the subject "The Attitude and Conduct of God's Servants." After introducing the topic, the teacher posed the question, "What then is an attitude?" The teacher did not look at anyone in particular for an answer. His eyes would dart up quickly from his booklet and then race back to it. Nobody offered an answer, so the teacher read the correct response from his edition of the lesson booklet. The teacher next asked the question, "What should the conduct and attitude of a Christian be?" After several moments, a man in the third row raised his hand. "We should show respect for our brothers and sisters." The teacher expressed agreement, adding, "Especially older members of the church, the elders, should be respected. Anything else?" The teacher stood behind a lectern, situated between the right and left sections of pews, without ever looking in the direction of women. Different male students volunteered the following comments: "The Christian should show reserve . . . good Christian reserve." "Have an attitude of humility." "Because none of us know all of the answers, we should appreciate all of our brothers."

The next question that the teacher raised to the group was, "What are some right ways to honor our church leaders?" The men offered a variety of answers to this question, including: "Appreciate what they stand for, what they teach." "Do not accuse leaders of wrongdoings without two or three witnesses." "Give them gifts." "Better to obey them than give gifts." "Allow them free time to work for the church." The teacher continued the lesson by asking a final question from the booklet. "How do we discern false teaching?" To this issue, students in the men's section provided four answers:

- If we know the truth of the Word, then we can plainly see the false.

- Something is false if it is contrary to the words of Christ.
- But, the red letter is not really enough . . . the black print is important too, all the way through the Epistles to Revelation.
- False teaching caters to the flesh . . . truth promotes godliness.

Expanding on the theme of "false teaching," the teacher directed the attention of his students to the following paragraph in the workbook:

> Money was not the only thing plentiful in Ephesus. Various religious influences needed to be guarded against as well. Greek mythology, worship of Diana, and a strong presence of Judaism were all part of the religious culture in Ephesus. Paul charged Timothy with the responsibility of combating these false teachers and their false ideas.

During Sunday School, I observed that most Eastern Mennonites take detailed notes on the lesson. They bring large Bibles along to class, with a writing utensil and plenty of paper. Their Bibles include both the Old and New Testaments, and some have the words of Jesus printed in red. Many of the books are kept in special vinyl jackets, with attached pockets to hold notepaper and a pen. If they bring anything at all to church with them, Weaverland Mennonites bring black, pocket-sized copies of the New Testament, printed only in black ink. I never observed a Weaverland Mennonite taking notes during sermons.

When the 45 minute period allowed for Sunday School is over, an obnoxious signal is given over the loudspeaker—a moment of loud static. At this signal, the adults stand up and quietly return to the pews they occupied before Sunday School. The children, in a quiet and orderly manner, come back into the auditorium and take their seats toward the front of the auditorium.

The Worship Service

When all of the children, young people, and adults have found their places in the auditorium, the bishop of the Eastern church stands up and greets the congregation. He opens his Bible and reads the most important verses from the Sunday School lesson. After a few comments about the reading, he asks for a volunteer to stand up and recite the week's memory verses. Normally, none of the members expresses an immediate interest in volunteering and the bishop, after assuming a look of disapproval, requests that everyone in the congregation say the verses together with him. The bishop starts the verse with a strong voice and the members of the congregation, speaking in unison, demonstrate that they have committed it to memory. After starting the exercise, the bishop closes his lips and with a stern expression, looks all around the group as if he were checking to see if anyone failed to memorize the scripture. At the end of the recitation, the bishop sits down in one of the front pews. In contrast to the Eastern Mennonites, Weaverlanders do not collectively read their Bibles or memorize verses during worship services. While the deacon reads the appointed text prior to the sermon, members listen but typically do not follow along in their own Bibles.

After the memory exercise, the deacon of the Eastern church stands up and welcomes any visitors who might be in the audience. He also announces upcoming congregational events. For example, on one Sunday I heard him mention that a "Singing Practice" had been scheduled, that another Eastern Mennonite Church would soon be ordaining a new deacon, and that the annual Summer Revival Meeting was beginning. When finished with announcements, the deacon takes his seat again. The Weaverland Mennonite Church does not organize revivals, tent meetings, or any other kind of "evening meeting." Whenever they get together to sing hymns, whether inside the church building, at Male Chorus, or at one another's homes, the event is never considered a "practice." The young people occasionally come together to learn new songs, but they do not rehearse them in an effort to sing better.

When it is time for the Eastern church to sing their first hymn, the songleader stands up behind a lectern and announces the name of the hymn, the book in which it may be found, and its page number. "We will begin this service by singing 'Spirit So Holy,' hymn number 133, *Christian Hymnal*." The songleader sings quietly into a microphone and uses his extended hand to keep tempo. The Eastern Mennonites use two different songbooks, which sit in shelves attached to the back of every pew. One of the books is called *The Christian Hymnal*, and the other is entitled *Church Hymnal*. Both of the hymnals include text and music for each song, notated with "shape notes." In contrast, the Weaverland hymnal includes only numbered texts, without musical notation. It is up to the songleader to set a fitting melody to the set of words selected. This means that the same text may be sung to different melodies. Sometimes a Weaverland songleader will make a mistake and choose a melody that does not structurally fit the text of the song— it might not have enough notes for each syllable of the text. On the few times that I observed this to happen, the congregation continued to sing until the end of the song. Among the Eastern Mennonites, a single songleader selects and begins all of the songs on a given Sunday. Among the Weaverlanders, however, a group of songleaders sit together at the Singer's Table and take turns starting hymns.

At the end of the first hymn, one of the Eastern ministers walks up to the front of the building and stands behind the raised pulpit, while the second minister sits down behind him on the raised pew. The first minister reads a portion of scripture and preaches a short sermon. One Sunday, for instance, the first minister read a chapter from the Gospel of Luke, concerning the "mighty power of faith the size of a mustard seed." He gave a brief lecture about how the Eastern Mennonites are "in this world to serve God's appointed purpose." He finished his talk by asking members to pray with him. Everyone in the congregation quickly turned to face the rear of the building, got down on their knees, and pressed their faces into the backrest of their pews. As he sank to his knees, the minister took the microphone with him. The prayer went on in silence for about 30 seconds, but was continued vocally by the minister. He petitioned on behalf of the sick, those lost in the world, and concluded by asking God to help members of the church be more faithful. When the prayer was over, the minister sat down on the raised pew.

After the first sermon, the Eastern Mennonite worship service continued with a second, somewhat longer sermon, preached by the other minister. On one particular Sunday I watched the second minister jump up to the pulpit and energetically proclaim the title of his sermon to be "The Holy Spirit of God":

> To help you with your outlines, I will tell you now that there are four parts to my lesson: Traits, Types, Titles, and Terms of the Spirit of God. But, first, I want you to know that the Holy Spirit is not an "It." It is wrong to say, "It moves among us." The Holy Spirit is not an It, not neuter. The Spirit is masculine; he is a "Him."

The sermon was very well organized and had a clear internal logic: the preacher's thoughts fell into categories, the categories fell neatly into order. Under the "Terms" section of his sermon, the minister described the "sealing of the Spirit, as found in Acts 4: 30." "This," he said, "is the same thing our sisters do when they can peaches. They want to protect the fruit from corruption by sealing it tightly."

The second minister normally preaches for about 25 minutes. His last comments come very close to a typical Protestant "altar call." He urges young people to come forward and join the church and reminds members of the need to publicly confess their sins. When he is finished and seated, the songleader leads a last song.

After the closing hymn and the songleader is back at his pew, the first minister leads a final prayer with all of the members standing. He holds his right hand near his ear during the prayer, a gesture of benediction not used by Weaverland ministers. This marks the end of the standard order of service at the Eastern Mennonite Church, consisting of two prayers, three songs, and two sermons.

The Weaverland ministers in New York State deliver their two back-to-back sermons in a very different manner. First, Weaverland ministers do not seem to organize their lessons prior to giving them. Their sermons appear to be products of free association, delivered impromptu as a stream of consciousness. I have never seen a Weaverland minister follow a previously written outline or notes. I have observed ministers apparently run out of things to say before their allotted time has expired. When this happens, a minister is likely to pick up a hymnal, select a song at random, and "line" it, reading the text out loud. If he does not discover something to comment on, he may pick another hymn or read from the Bible.

A certain minister for the Weaverland Mennonite Church had a particularly difficult time preaching coherent sermons. For many weeks after he had been chosen to fill the vacancy, he could not bring himself to preach in front of the congregation. Standing behind the preacher's table, this man would begin a sentence, stutter, become silent, and sob beyond control. After one particularly tearful sermon, a young Weaverland boy explained, facetiously, that the minister had "cried because his cows hadn't given enough milk this morning." When I asked an older member of the church what he thought about the new minister and his difficulties, I was told that young ministers often have problems adjusting to their new role, but that they eventually learn to fulfill their responsibilities.

When the worship service is concluded, both Weaverland and Eastern Mennonites tend to remain in the auditorium and visit with one another. At both churches, men and women speak in segregated groups of the same sex. During this time, the members of the Eastern church approach visitors and engage them in conversation. After introducing themselves, members typically ask visitors if they belong to another church or if they are "spiritual." The first time I visited, for instance, one of the ministers bluntly inquired as to the health of my soul. Easterners thank visitors for coming, suggest that they take home one or two of the religious tracts from the wall, and tell them that they would be happy to see them come again. Visitors are often invited to come home with a member and have lunch. With the exception of their traveling relatives, Weaverland Mennonites rarely have visitors to their church.

Members Talk About the Two Churches

No Eastern Mennonites have joined the Weaverland community, but Weaverlanders are joining the Easterners. I interviewed former members of the Weaverland church and learned some of the reasons why they converted to the Eastern Mennonites. Among their replies were the following complaints against the Weaverland church: "They don't let their light shine." "They are hopelessly stuck in the past." "We wanted a more open group, one where members could talk and really learn about the gospel of Jesus Christ."

New members of the Eastern Mennonites generally agreed that they wanted a more "evangelistic," "modern," and "dynamic" congregation. Some members had more specific reasons for being attracted to the Eastern church, for example:

> I prefer this seating arrangement. It's better for the family to sit together. Of course the men and women are still separate, which is good. But fathers are with their sons and mothers with their daughters. In the Horning [Weaverland] church, the adults and children are too far apart. It's hard to keep the younger children quiet that way—or even when they get too quiet and need some-

one to keep them awake, you're too far away to give a
nudge.

Another former Weaverlander reported, "Women are permitted to contribute to Sunday School discussions in this conference,
something that we missed in the old church." Most of the members
interviewed mentioned that they preferred a church with Sunday
School. As one man put it:

> You attend church your whole life without really grow-
> ing in the faith, never developing an appetite for more
> than spiritual milk. Christians can't live on that. Sunday
> school is a necessary part of the missionary effort. When
> people ask you what you are about, it's necessary to
> have an answer ready so that your beliefs and practices
> can be explained.

When I asked one of the Eastern Mennonite ministers, a former Weaverlander, to explain why he believed Weaverlanders
might be joining his conference, he stated, "Many of their members
run to us because they need a living church."

Some Weaverland members reported that they occasionally
visited the Eastern Mennonites, but for various reasons were not
willing to join. According to one informant,

> We don't make a point of letting people know that we like
> many of the things that they do [the Eastern Mennonites].
> But my family enjoys visiting when we go, especially the
> children. They really like Sunday School. As a songleader
> [with the Weaverland church], I think that their hymnal
> is nicer than ours, with the notes and all. There are rea-
> sons why we would like to join, but one thing certainly
> holds us back. The family is all here [among the Weaver-
> land members], we could not leave them.

Another Weaverlander suggested that the appeal of the Eastern Mennonite Church for some people is only temporary:

> I understand why some of us are going over there, but I can tell you that most will be back. You know that the Henry Zimmermans have already come back, so have others. The fact is that group is outright nasty to everybody outside of its walls. They think that everyone who is not a member of their little conference is going to hell.
>
> They are even nasty to their own members. They expelled a 16-year-old boy for getting a simple speeding ticket. Repentance was not possible, because the church was publicly embarrassed. That is terrible! They also have a habit of silencing their ministers. As soon as one of them says something the others don't like, he gets silenced. It is not a loving congregation!

When asked to comment about the Eastern church and its attraction for Weaverland members, a Weaverland minister gave the following response:

> For more than a year now, the Eastern church has needed to replace a minister that they expelled. However, they won't have a selection because the old Eastern members think that the chances are too high that a new member [formerly] from our conference will draw the lot. They would rather do without the new minister than risk having an "impure" Weaverlander take the position. That should show you the mentality of that group. But it also shows you that we are losing too many members to them.

In the opinion of another member of the Weaverland community, the two Old Order churches have similar beliefs but "apply" them in different ways. Despite the differences that exist between the two groups, some members actually exchange the Kiss of Charity.

It is understandable that ill feelings may arise between churches when one seems to be gaining members from the other. However there is little difference in our faith. Applications do vary but I do believe that very few Eastern Mennonites would believe that anyone not belonging to their group is lost. We need to take greater care in not allowing bad attitudes to overwhelm us.

Explaining the Attraction of the Eastern Mennonite Church

In his comparative sociology of religion, Max Weber (1972; 1988) introduced several descriptive concepts that are effective tools for understanding the social features of different religious groups. His analytic concept of "rationalization" is particularly useful for describing the extent that a religion has systematized its beliefs and "demystified" itself (1972: 308). Weber maintained that priests are primarily responsible for steering the laity away from emotional rituals and magic, towards a consistent creed and corresponding ethos. With increasing rationalization, priests become professional leaders of the group (1972: 279–304), the membership tends to express orthodox beliefs (1972: 281), and religious values are articulated so that they do not interfere with material concerns (1972: 311; 1988: 567).

I believe that the Eastern Mennonite Conference may be attracting Weaverland Mennonites because it is, in Weber's sense, a more rational church. In the Eastern Mennonite Church, ministers are better trained and have a more specialized role as religious functionaries, intellectualization of the congregation is enhanced through Sunday School, there is an active effort to evangelize the world, and members are not discouraged from taking up a wide variety of non-farming occupations. Because they now interact more frequently with people who are unfamiliar with their life-style and who present alternative ways of thinking and living, Weaverland Mennonites in New York State have an increased interest in learning how to rationally account for their Old Order traditions and beliefs. The Eastern Mennonite Church supplies products that meet this demand: specialized ministers, well-organized sermons, Sunday School, propaganda literature, and a church building that nonmembers are able to recognize as such.

Compared with the Weaverland church building, the Eastern building reflects greater rationalization in two ways. First, there are many architectural contrivances in the Eastern church that focus the attention of the congregation on the pulpit, toward the ministers: front-facing pews, a large conspicuous pulpit situated on a raised platform, spotlights, microphones, an attractive scenery behind the front windows, etc. Second, the fixtures and furnishings are more "mainstream"; they could be found in just about any church—except in a traditional Old Order building. The songbooks, carpet, informative tracts, microphones, elevated pulpit, and other items demonstrate that the Easterners are willing to change the physical appearance of the traditional Old Order church. Many of these items were purchased from businesses that market standard, interdenominational "church supplies." These artifacts of the group's material culture, most notably the "Visitors Welcome" sign outside the building, create the impression that the Eastern Mennonites are a "typical" Protestant congregation. Most of the furnishings inside the Weaverland church were handmade by members—they are simple and reflect a singular aesthetic ideal. Unlike the plain Weaverland building, the Eastern church looks much like a rural Baptist or Methodist church.

Weaverland Mennonites in New York strive to live in isolation from the world; it is safe to say that they lead a life of "world-negating asceticism" (Weber 1972: 329). As a consequence, the church

is not concerned with conducting missionary work.[5] In contrast,
the Eastern Mennonites support a wide variety of evangelistic operations. Not only do they distribute religious pamphlets to people
who visit their services, but also they disseminate such literature
in public—at shopping centers, for instance. The tracts defend
their religious practices and beliefs. Visitors to church are politely
but aggressively invited for lunch in members' homes after services. After the meal, visitors are interviewed about their spiritual
welfare and are asked to come back again. I regularly attended the
Weaverland church for more than a year before a member invited
me home for lunch after church. Eastern Mennonites visit local
colleges and "spread the Gospel," participate in international Mennonite missions, and donate money to relief agencies. Consistent
with Weber's portrayal of the "inner-worldly ascetic," the Eastern
Mennonite considers himself God's instrument on earth, actively
working to reform the world.

    If one evaluates them as teachers who have the goal of edu-
cating people, the untrained Weaverland ministers do not preach
as effectively as their counterparts in the Eastern church. While

*Figure 8.1. Unlike the Weaverland Mennonites, the Eastern Mennonites
distribute many different informational tracts in order to explain their
religious beliefs and practices to "the World."*

the Weaverland preachers are not trained in church doctrine or homiletics, new Eastern preachers must go through a brief training program. In one important detail, the selection process for ministers is different for the two churches. When forming a class of candidates to fill a vacant position, the Weaverland congregation allows each member to nominate a person. Assuming that they meet the religious qualifications to do so, an individual may "share the lot" if they receive one vote. The Eastern church has increased the number of votes required to become a candidate to four. This may be considered a more rational procedure, as it requires more members to agree that a certain person has the necessary qualifications to fill a leadership position.

While Eastern members take notes during the sermon and follow along in their own Bibles, Weaverlanders sit still and listen, while not just a few doze off in slumber. I once looked at a full pew in the boys' section and found that more people were asleep than awake. During one particularly dull Weaverland sermon, a young boy fell off his pew while dozing. After making an exceptionally loud noise upon hitting the wood floor, he got up, sat back down, and fell asleep again. As one member told me, "This is an embarrassing situation. It is probably a combination of long working days and not enough enthusiasm in the church services. Sleeping in church is not an accepted practice across the Weaverland Mennonite churches." Acceptable or not, it is not uncommon to hear adults snoring and babies crying during the Weaverland service. The Eastern Mennonites, however, have ushers that nudge sleepers and escort crying babies, with their mothers, to the nursery in the foyer.

One of the most significant reasons for the schism that gave rise to the Weaverland Conference was that Mennonites in the Lancaster General Conference could not agree on the institution of Sunday Schools. The majority of the members wanted to adopt the institution, as practiced by local Protestant churches. The reactionary minority, led by bishop Jonas Martin, split off and formed the Weaverland Conference (see Schlabach 1985: 226–29). One hundred years later, the Weaverland Conference is still opposed to organized religious education:

> In response to those people who have expressed an interest in Sunday schools, the oldest bishop advised several years ago that the children should be taught the Bible and that anyone who wishes can have Sunday school—at home in their own kitchen. (Martin and Martin 1985: 70)

Theron F. Schlabach (1985: 228) notes that the opponents of Sunday School failed to realize that "loyal Mennonites" might use it to teach "separatism, nonconformity, nonresistance, and other Mennonite principles. They seem not to have realized that Sunday Schools could become transmitters and defenders of the Mennonite faith." J.C. Wenger (1966: 167) observed that one of the "major purposes" of Sunday School eventually became the preservation of the German language.

With their Sunday School program for all ages, the Eastern Mennonite Church offers a wide variety of lessons tailored to the special needs of different groups. Small children sing songs, hear stories, and color pictures depicting biblical heroes and scenes. Teenagers learn what it means to join the church and live as members. Young adults are taught church doctrine and how to select friends and spouses. Adults read the Bible and discuss interpretations. Every class has a separate workbook, published by "experts" that specialize in teaching Christianity. The books are designed so that a new lesson is taught every Sunday, systematically covering a great variety of fundamental topics over the year. Using an entirely different framework, Weaverland members, young and old, all hear the same sermon, without having any forum for discussion.

Karl Mannheim (1982: 336) suggested that there are different ways that social groups generate and reproduce shared ideas about how members ought to exist in the world. Fitting one of Mannheim's descriptions, the Weaverlanders construct their world-view through a process of democratic consensus. Each member possesses relatively the same information pertaining to what it means to be Mennonite and how "proper" Mennonites ought to behave. The bishop, preachers, and deacons are nominated by the congregation and fulfill their roles without special training or priv-ileged information. According to Mannheim, this kind of egalitari-an "ownership" of the collective consciousness can only work under static conditions—when traditional and established ways of thought may easily be used again and again. There are no spiritual experts or specialists in the Weaverland community.

Fitting a different type described by Mannheim, the Eastern Mennonites have given guardianship of their worldview to their ministers. The ministers enjoy what Mannheim called an "intellec-tual monopoly" of the group's worldview (1982: 338). They teach a systematic theology, distribute approved educational materials, and speak through a microphone under a spotlight. It is not sur-prising that Eastern ministers have greater personal authority over congregational affairs than Weaverland ministers. According to Weber, Sunday School and other educational programs are typical-ly used by priests to gain organizational control over their church-es (1988: 565). Emphasizing its effectiveness in socializing young people, Thompson (1986: 78–79) also discussed Sunday School as a means to social control.

Weber (1972) and Mannheim (1982) agreed that with priests and their intellectual monopoly come dogma and orthodoxis, and these fuel competition in the spiritual realm. "With [dogma] the need arises to differentiate oneself from competitive outside teach-ings and to use propaganda to stay in control" (Weber 1972: 281). But why do religious people turn their attention to priests, dogma, and orthodoxis in the first place? In the case of the Weaverland Mennonites who migrated from "Pennsylvania Dutch Country" to New York State, I believe that members found themselves surrounded by people who lived different life-styles from their own and who had no prior experience with "Plain People." Consequently, Old Order behavior could no longer be taken for granted—by members or nonmembers. Adjusting Weber and Mannheim's thesis, I think that members of a religious group are first attracted to dogma, orthodoxis, and the priests that create them once they begin to interact with members of other groups who do not share their norms and values.

While Weaverland Mennonites who migrated to New York State intended to construct a new Plain community modeled after those in Pennsylvania, with the same church regulations and a commitment to an agricultural life-style, one very significant characteristic is peculiar to the new settlement. Inside the 550 square mile region in which members of the new community have bought farms, there is only *one member of the church per four square miles.* In contrast, the Weaverland Conference of Old Order Mennonites has 14 individual church buildings located inside the 400 square mile area north of Lancaster, Pennsylvania. Each of the congregations in Pennsylvania contains an average of 140 members, resulting in a population density of *five members per square mile.* In their search for the most attractive farms they could find in New York State, families isolated themselves geographically. Consequently, members of the new church rarely see each other during the week, using their black-bumper cars to commute back to the community each Sunday for worship.

Living in isolation from other members of the church and interacting daily with their new worldly neighbors, I believe that many Weaverland Mennonites came to an uncomfortable realization—they could not intelligently explain to themselves or to other people why they adhere to their religious traditions. This realization brought about an appetite for trained ministers, dogma, and orthodoxis. Untrained "lay" ministers could not supply Weaverland Mennonites with satisfying explanations. With regard to their religious tradition, the untrained Weaverland ministers know little more than other members. Such an egalitarian distribution of religious knowledge is only effective as long as members take the legitimacy of their traditional behaviors for granted.

Comparing the Eastern and Weaverland Mennonite churches with the help of Weber's concept of "rationalization" is illuminating as it highlights qualities that enable the Easterners to attract members away from the Weaverland Conference. The egalitarian leadership of untrained ministers, a more passive worship service, the rejection of Sunday School and formal religious education, and an unwillingness to discuss religious doctrine as a group are qualities of the Weaverland congregation that make it less rationalized— decreasing its competitiveness and power to keep members in a new social setting. Since Weaverland Mennonites have not endeavored to articulate their theology in generalizable terms, with a vocabulary of accounts that do not remain self-referential, members are less able to meaningfully communicate with nonmembers when asked to account for their religious practices and beliefs. Successful communication with nonmembers is increasingly important for members of both the Eastern and Weaverland Churches who, as a consequence of their migration to New York State, interact more with their new worldly neighbors than with people who share their social and religious traditions.

Though they are all aware of the Eastern Mennonite Church, not all Weaverland Mennonites think about it in the same way. Some have already converted to the other church, some plan to do so in the future, a few confess that they would like to go but probably never will, and still others would never consider leaving the Weaverland Conference. However, whatever their thoughts regarding the Eastern Mennonite Church, Weaverland Mennonites continue to conform to church regulations and uniformly participate in ritual activities.

Notes

1. *A Collection of Psalms and Hymns* 1977: 296.

2. The Eastern Pennsylvania Mennonite Church broke away from the Mennonite Church's Lancaster Conference after an "amiable" schism during the years 1968–69 (see Graber 1984). Those who favored starting the more conservative church claimed that they desired a stricter discipline and more actively evangelistic relationship with the world.

3. Outside of New York State, some Weaverland congregations do use microphones. As one member explained: "Several years ago the Conference ruled that if the caretakers and the Deacons of a given Church (within the entire Weaverland Conference) agree on the need for a loud speaker system, it may be installed, providing it can be done peacefully. There are at least seven of the (Weaverland) churches with (public address) systems installed now."

4. In the opinion of one Weaverlander, "There is no significance in the fit of the curtains except that if they do not fit well, someone did not fit them properly."

5. Some Weaverland members do participate in missionary programs organized by other Mennonite Conferences.

Chapter 9

Conclusion: Doing the Same Things for Different Reasons

Mid scenes of confusion and creature complaints,
How sweet to my soul is communion with saints,
To find at the banquet of mercy there's room,
And feel in the presence of Jesus, at home.[1]

In his pioneering study in the sociology of religion, *The Elementary Forms of the Religious Life* (1965), Emile Durkheim emphasized the significance that a sacred sign or totem has for an association of people. According to Durkheim, "A clan is essentially a reunion of individuals who bear the same name and rally around the same sign. Take away the sign which materializes it, and the clan is no longer representable" (1965: 265). By identifying themselves with the same signs, the Weaverland Old Order Mennonites of New York State have symbolically built a community. United under a common symbol, individual members can see themselves and present themselves in the social world as an integrated group. Their common name and sign unites them in opposition to other groups that they desire to be distinguished from.

The Weaverland Old Order Mennonites examined in this book have created a system of signs that powerfully represent themselves as a visible community. The Conference Reports function to clearly mark the difference between a member and a non-member of the church. As long as they live their lives in conformity to the Rules of the Church, members may participate in collective religious rituals such as Communion and the Washing of Feet. They are also entitled to share the social and economic rewards of membership. By taking up the signs of membership and engaging in social rituals, each individual Mennonite demonstrates that he or she is an authentic member of the Weaverland community. "The reality and efficacy of the community's boundary—and, therefore, of the community itself—depends upon its symbolic construction and embellishment" (Cohen 1985: 15).

If they identify with a common name, use the same signs, and perform collective rituals together, do the members of a social group such as the Weaverland Mennonites necessarily share collective beliefs? Do they each understand the meaning of their name in the same manner and attach the same interpretations to their signs and rituals? Do members of a symbolic community understand the meaning of their sign in the same manner? When I first observed Weaverland Mennonites interacting with each other, I was impressed with the apparent similarities between individual members. I observed a remarkable uniformity in the appearance and behavior of members. When I attended church services, I was struck by the orderliness, regularity, and predictability of Mennonite rituals. I assumed that Weaverlanders conformed to the Conference Rules and engaged in rituals in order to act out their *common* religious beliefs. However, after I had become more familiar with Weaverland Mennonites, I realized that members often acted in concert *without* attaching the same religious beliefs—or any kind of belief—to their collective behavior.

As I explained in chapter 6, members of the Weaverland community who do not use the appropriate signs of membership or who do not participate in the rituals of the group are excommunicated. Members know how they are expected to behave and they generally conform. Hence, it is very rare that the church must expel a member. As discussed in chapter 5, the *Confession of Faith* (1996) booklet explicitly describes how members should perform Mennonite rituals. Behavioral standards for everyday life are specified in the "Church Discipline." I believe that the prescriptions and proscriptions included in these two documents, established as tradition and enforced by the sanction of expulsion, effectively maintain orthopraxis within the community.

For Weaverland Mennonites, orthopraxis appears to occur without orthodoxis. That is, members may engage in the same "correct" behavior, but explain the significance of the behavior in different voices—a "correct" interpretation is not uniformly supplied. I first discussed this phenomenon in chapter 1, in reference to the Kiss of Peace. The Mennonites seem to demonstrate that participation in a "religious" ritual does not require that all of the actors define the situation in the same manner, share a world view, or that actors attach the same meaning to an action. In fact, ritual interaction can occur even when one or more of the participants does not understand the significance of the action or is thinking about a mundane, completely unrelated matter. *Religious action, as when members of a congregation appear to follow church regulations or engage in rituals, has been shown here to not depend on the existence of a shared set of religious beliefs, but on a shared recognition of and conformity to established rules of behavior.* As long as they adhere to such rules and contribute to a "good show," the personal beliefs of Weaverland members are never questioned.

In this final chapter, I summarize my observations of the Weaverland Mennonites in New York State. I critically evaluate two assumptions commonly held by sociologists of religion. First, I reject the notion that members of a religious group are integrated because they share beliefs. Second, I also reject the claim that religious communities perform rituals in order to enact previously established collective beliefs. Religion is a source of social unity only as long as people are willing to submit their personal beliefs to the common symbol. The religious conduct of Weaverland Mennonites is governed—directed, guided, and regulated—by the *Confession of Faith* and the Rules of the Church. The symbols and rituals of Weaverland Mennonites sustain unity in the group because they completely transcend the individual beliefs of members.

From my perspective, religious beliefs do not necessarily play a significant role in creating congregational solidarity. Religious rituals, symbols, and signs unite members of a congregation even if individuals do not attach the same significance to them. Members of a church may assume that they believe the same things, and they may even endeavor to establish an orthodox creed and require affirmation to it. A heretic, however, may also be compelled to affirm the official creed. All over the world, people stand together and recite creeds, promises, and prayers in languages that they do not understand. In the United States, for instance, school children are expected to recite the Pledge of Allegiance every morning—but nobody expects them to be able to explain the words they use. To be socially meaningful, a symbol, ritual, or collective celebration does not need to have a single meaning.

According to A.P. Cohen (1985: 16), "When we speak of people acquiring culture, or learning to be social, we mean that they acquire the symbols which will equip them to be social." Symbols, Cohen maintains, "do not tell us *what* to mean, but give us the capacity to make meaning." In the construction of community, members depend on rituals and symbols for the simple reason that their own personal beliefs cannot equip them to be social. Individuals cannot change the fact that their thoughts remain hidden away in the mind. As expressed in a German song popular among those who resisted Hitler, "*Die Gedanken sind frei, wer kann sie erraten*" (Thoughts are free, who can guess them). The most penetrating inquisitor cannot be certain that a person truly believes in the established creed.

Weaverland Mennonites enforce collective conformity to group practices, but rarely seem concerned about regulating conformity to group beliefs. I believe this is because Mennonites understand that the only effective test of authentic membership in the church is one's conduct. "By their *works* shall ye know them." From a pragmatic perspective, as long as members follow the rules of the church, their personal reasons for doing so are of little social consequence.

Can Members of a Community Share Beliefs?

The anthropologist Robert Redfield (1947: 293–97) was convinced that the members of "traditional" communities share the same beliefs. As a matter of fact, Redfield suggested that a social scientist investigating a "folk society" could learn "what all men know and believe" by learning "what goes on in the minds of a few of its members," perhaps even from a single member. Though the Weaverland Mennonite community studied here does exhibit the typical characteristics of Redfield's "folk society," the "mechanical society" (Durkheim 1964), and the "*Gemeinshaft*" (Toennies 1963), I have found that its members give very diverse explanations for their collective actions, if they give any at all. Indeed, to account for their religious behavior, the most common "statement of belief" among members of the Weaverland group is "That's just the way we do it."

What would it mean to claim that the members of a group share a belief? What would have to take place before a collectively held belief could come into existence? Margaret Gilbert (1989), a philosopher who focuses on social relations, has commented insightfully on these questions. According to Gilbert, there are a few typical arguments that are generally used to support the claim "group G believes p." In this case, "p" signifies a specific propositional statement. For example, "p" might stand for the belief that "Christians should drive black cars because black shows humility." First, there is a "summative" argument in which it is asserted, "Group G believes p" because "most of its members believe p." One problem with this argument is that individuals who are clearly not members of G may also believe p. That is, sharing a belief in p does not necessarily involve membership in G. Furthermore, many active members of G may not believe in p. Some members may not have realized that as members of G, they are expected to believe p. Nonetheless, these members may be, in everyday life, identified as authentic members of G.

One might argue that group G believes p because a special minority of members of G believes p. For instance, most Mennonites may not be able to explain why they believe it is necessary to drive black automobiles, but they do assume that their ministers could explain why. Thus, one might assert that Mennonites have a certain collective belief because they assume that their ministers have a certain collective belief. When I would ask Weaverlanders to tell me about their religious beliefs, I was frequently told that I should "ask one of the ministers." As observed by Clyde Kluckhohn (1949: 32), "No amount of questioning of any save the most articulate in the most self-conscious cultures will bring out some of the basic attitudes common to the members of the group. This is because these basic assumptions are so taken for granted that they normally do not enter consciousness." Following this argument, one could suggest that the only propositional statement that Mennonites collectively accept is that their ministers share beliefs: We all believe the same thing, and though we cannot tell you what we all believe, we all know that the preacher could tell you if you needed to know. Because Weaverland Ministers are selected by lot from the membership and serve the church without any theological training, it seems unreasonable to expect them to have a special understanding of "Mennonite beliefs." Even if the ministers did share a common and orthodox understanding of "Mennonite" beliefs, this would not mean that Mennonites, as a group, have a collective understanding of beliefs.

Would it make sense to claim that Mennonites, as a group, have a collective belief even if no single member of the church has the belief? Gilbert explains the subtle logic of this "nonsummative" account for collective belief:

> Once a certain point is reached, a given view is established as the group view, and this could remain the group view even if everyone subsequently came to have a contrary personal opinion. Hence, the group can believe something at a certain point in time without any member of the group believing it. Moreover, it appears not to be necessary that any member of the group ever believed it. Suppose everyone lets one person's suggestion stand unopposed and hence it establishes the group's view. The person in question need not have believed what she said. A variety of motivations could lie behind her saying something she disbelieved or about which she had no current opinion. (1989: 290)

Even if no member of the church personally accepts a particular belief, we may still claim that Mennonites share that belief, as long as members know that, as Mennonites, they are expected to accept that collective belief. As Gilbert suggests,

> The [nonsummative] account proposed does not require that anyone explicitly agrees to anything. Evidently one can communicate one's willingness to participate in joint acceptance in quite subtle, nonverbal ways. It will be understood in advance that one has intentionally and openly expressed such willingness, they do jointly accept that p. *Thus joint acceptance can be brought about without explicit recognition of what has taken place.* (1989: 307; emphasis added)

Immediately before joining their church through baptism, Weaverland Mennonites participate in a mandatory program of "instruction." For nine weeks, as I related in chapter 3, the young people meet after Sunday services with members of the ministry. During each session, two articles of faith from the *Confession of Faith of the Mennonite* (1996) are read aloud. There is very little discussion about the meaning of each article of faith and no formal attempt is made by the ministry to test whether or not students have understood or memorized the articles of belief. It is assumed, however, that the young adults who join the church have adopted the beliefs that Mennonites are expected to share.

Calvin Redekop (1969) conducted an investigation of Old Colony Mennonites in Mexico and observed how young people were "taught" what members of the church ought to believe. Like the Weaverland Mennonites of New York State, the Old Colony Mennonites clearly demonstrate that a group may believe that members share beliefs, even if individual members do not understand what they are supposed to believe. Redekop found that young people who desire to join an Old Colony congregation must study their group's beliefs well enough to pass a ceremonial review:

When the applicants have successfully "understood" the catechism, they are presented to the congregation on a Sunday morning. The minister asks them to rise and answer in order the questions studied in class. The object of the ceremony is to recite his answers flawlessly. For the congregation, the object is to see how well the applicants have learned their catechism. "The saying of the catechism is the very important event. It is the thing the young people dread most. Most young people memorize it by rote, not knowing what is going on as far as meaning is concerned." (P. 58)

Among the Weaverland and Old Colony Mennonites, each young person is expected to openly confirm his or her acceptance of the group's religious doctrine. Through the ritual of baptism, each individual member communicates his or her acceptance of the collective "Confession of Faith." Even if members do not understand the meaning of the articles that comprise the official confession, they publicly affirm that they accept the collective beliefs of their congregation.

I believe that Weaverland Mennonites do not explain their symbolic behavior in an orthodox manner for a simple reason. Shared beliefs do not exist until they are created, and this process is complex. A collectively held belief would have to be invented, articulated, adopted, disseminated, and constantly protected against alternative beliefs (Zito 1983). A shared belief is artificial and cannot arise without this active and creative process—it is a social construction and must be propagated. Weaverland Mennonites do not demonstrate orthodoxis because they have not made a concerted effort to produce it.

It is not enough to say that Mennonites have a collective belief because they all know that their automobiles must be painted black. In this case, one could claim that a collective belief exists only after demonstrating that each individual gives the same reasons when asked to explain why Weaverland Mennonites drive black cars. For this to be possible members would have to work together to codify and adopt an orthodox statement of belief to support the prescription for black cars: our cars must be black because we believe that p. As I discussed in chapter 7, when the validity of a social rule is called into question, members of society are pressed to give an account to defend its legitimacy. If Black Bumper Mennonites agree that p is the reason that they paint their cars black, whatever p actually means, then it may be claimed that they have a collective belief. If the members of a group do give the same account for a common practice, one may safely assume that they have taken trouble to establish such unlikely uniformity. But even if members do recite the same "nonsummative account" for a rule, one may not assume that any member sincerely believes what they are professing. The giving of an account, the act of stating "one's belief," may also turn into a socially meaningful ritual that has little personal significance for participants. A traitor can also swear allegiance.

Weaverland Mennonites in New York State do not make a habit of reading their *Confession of Faith* book, they do not evangelize or formally teach doctrine, and they do not openly discuss one another's beliefs. How can we expect the members of this church to share collective beliefs if they have not endeavored to create them? There is simply no such thing as "a *Mennonite* belief." There are only Mennonites who claim to have beliefs. Members of this religious community typically take for granted that sound spiritual reasons exist to support each of their practices or rules. Weaverland Mennonites are unlikely to feel the need to construct a system of orthodox beliefs until they can no longer take the existence of shared beliefs for granted. In the preceding chapter, I discussed how increased interaction with "people of the world" has apparently created this need for some Weaverlanders.

Can Members of a Group Be Integrated Without Sharing Beliefs?

Durkheim suggested that religion provides individuals with "an active reason to fraternize," by creating "the same spirit which animates all minds. And all this in such a way as to weaken the distinction between me and you, mine and yours" (cited in Wallwork 1985: 214). He believed that the members of a social group are united by a "collective conscience," which is comprised of the moral rules and beliefs they commonly accept. Each person has his or her own conscience—guidelines for living and personal beliefs. Yet, members of society also possess a collective conscience, "one which is shared in common with our group in its entirety, which, consequently, is not ourself, but society living and acting within us" (cited in Wallwork 1972: 38).

In *The Elementary Forms of the Religious Life* (1965), Durkheim explained how the individual members of a society come to share religious beliefs or "collective representations":

> We have considered the religious representations as if they were self-sufficient and could be explained by themselves. But in reality, they are inseparable from the rites, not only because they manifest themselves there, but also because they, in their turn, feel the influence of these. Of course the cult depends upon the beliefs, but it also reacts upon them. (P. 333, see also p. 121)

How do rituals influence beliefs if they cannot exist without them? Durkheim believed that during the religious ritual, or the "cult," individuals recognize the power of their social union, creating a special mood of "collective effervescence." Jane Ellen Harrison, a student of ancient Greek religion, well described the collective ecstasy created by ritual:

A high emotional tension is best caused and maintained
by a thing felt socially. The individual in a savage tribe
has but a thin and meager personality. If he dances
alone he will not dance long; but if his whole tribe
dances together, he will dance the live-long night and
his emotion will mount to passion, to ecstasy. . . . Emotion socialized, felt collectively, is emotion intensified
and rendered permanent. Intellectually the group is
weak. . . . Emotionally the group is strong; everyone
knows this who has felt the thrill of speaking to or acting with a great multitude. (1912: 43)

In this ebullient state, experienced only during ritual, Durkheim
suggested that new beliefs and ideas might spring into existence.

Durkheim believed that rituals are the enactments of collectively held beliefs, but that rituals create the shared ecstasy
required for the formulation and affirmation of those beliefs.

There can be no society which does not feel the need of
upholding and reaffirming at regular intervals the collective sentiments and the collective ideas which make
its unity and its personality. Now this moral remaking
cannot be achieved except by the means of reunions,
assemblies and meetings where the individuals, being
closely united to one another, reaffirm in common their
common sentiments; hence come ceremonies that do
not differ from regular religious ceremonies, either in
their object, the results they produce, or the processes
employed to attain these results. (1964: 474–75)

According to Durkheim, "collective sentiments" and "collective
ideas" produce the "unity" of every social group. *Though
Durkheim understood that ritual behavior may create new*

beliefs, he was convinced that rituals "manifest" previously established collective representations. This aspect of Durkheim's approach to ritual and belief is put into question by the religious activity of Weaverland Mennonites. The members of this community participate in common rituals *but* attach different meanings to them. I find that Weaverlanders take for granted that they hold the same beliefs, when in fact they do not. Nevertheless, this "definition of the situation" has the real consequence of social integration. When it comes to social solidarity, what matters most of all is not *what is* but *what people believe is.* With his proposition that collective beliefs necessarily stand behind collective action, Durkheim failed to understand that the members of a group can identify with the same name, adopt the same signs of membership, and engage in ritual behavior without having the same sentiments or beliefs. I am not suggesting that individual actors do not personally attach spiritual significance to their ritual behavior. However, my observations of Weaverland Mennonites lead me to reject the notion that participants in collective ritual must attach *the same significance* to their actions or that actors in ritual always think about "what they ought to be thinking about."

Symbols, rituals, emblems, and names are powerful sources of social integration even if the members of a group do not attach the same meaning, motivation, or interpretation to them. Individuals are united in a community because they share signs and rituals, but they may share these things without sharing their meanings. "That one may smile, and smile, and be a villain!" (Hamlet I:v: 109). In his study of how symbols are used to construct community, Cohen (1985) maintained that:

> Culture, constituted by symbols, does not impose itself in such a way as to determine that all its adherents should make the same sense of the world. Rather, it merely gives them the capacity to make sense and, if they tend to

make a similar kind of sense, it is not because of any deterministic influence but because they are doing so with the same symbols. The quintessential referent of community is that its members make, or believe they make, a similar sense of things . . . that they think that sense may differ from one made elsewhere . . . . The reality of community in people's experience inheres in their attachment or commitment to a common body of symbols. . . . But it must be emphasized that the sharing of symbol is not necessarily the same as the sharing of meaning. (Pp. 15–16)

The Relationship Between the Rituals and Beliefs of Weaverland Mennonites

In chapter 5, I described how members of the Weaverland community observe three of their most important religious rituals twice each year. On a special Sunday in spring and autumn, the members gather to perform the ordinances of the Lord's Supper, Washing of Feet, and the Holy Kiss. These rituals are highly scripted, programmed enactments that are repeated in the same manner year after year. The rites involve unusually intimate physical contact between members, spoken exchanges, special props, and highly regulated movements of the body. Every member participates according to the established script, acting out a part in the ritual that conforms to group expectations.

These rituals are complicated social interactions that require participants to adhere to rules of conduct. Worshipers must silently stand at one point, kneel and shut their eyes at another point, utter a memorized prayer next, and close the ritual by kissing the person next to them in a precisely defined manner. All actors are expected to follow the rules of ritual participation, according to the role that they are assigned. The women do one thing, the men another; the bishop does this, the preacher that, and the deacon something else; the children sit quietly and watch, learning through observation the rules that they will eventually follow. If procedural rules are followed correctly, a ritual can be successfully performed even if actors do not share an understanding of its spiritual significance. *Indeed, if such understanding were ever created, procedural rules would still have to be constructed before a rite could be enacted.* Actors do not even need to know how to verbalize or formulate the rules that they follow (Winch 1977: 58). Among students of religion, the concept of ritual is usually conceived of as an already completed act. Real participants also tend to speak of "whole" rituals: observing "communion" or "footwashing." As Alfred Schutz (1967: 61) wrote, "the actor projects his action as if it were already over and done with and lying in the past." Nevertheless, thinking about a ritual as if it were a monolithic act obscures its fragmented nature:

> When an interpretive sociologist examines an action, he assumes that it has unity and that this can be defined. Yet in practice, when he comes to relate observational and motivational understanding, he defines the action arbitrarily, without reference to the intended meaning of the actor. If the goal is given, the means follows, and each means then becomes an intermediate goal which must be accomplished by still other means. The total act thus divides into component acts, and an external observer who is "objectively" watching such a series of "component" acts is in no position to say whether the goal has yet been reached or whether there is more to come. Each component stage can be regarded as a new unity. (Schutz 1967: 62)

Every ritual is comprised of numerous components, frames that are necessary for the act to become whole and successful. For example, during communion there is a time to kneel, to sing, to drink, and a time to open one's mouth for bread. The frames must all fall in the proper order: nobody sings while chewing or kneels while drinking. The procedural rules published in the *Confession of Faith* ensure that the ritual frames fall correctly into place in their appropriate sequence.

As with language, ritual is only meaningful when it conforms to established rules of structure. Participants in both conversation and ritual must use appropriate grammar and syntax in order to meaningfully interact. Peter Winch argued "that the analysis of meaningful behavior must allot a central role to the notion of a rule; that all behavior which is meaningful (therefore all specifically human behavior) is *ipso facto* rule-governed" (1977: 51–52). Ferdinand de Saussere (1966), the French linguist, maintained that individuals can only communicate by expressing themselves systematically; when they understand and correctly follow the established rules of a linguistic system. Language is a social construction created when signs are arbitrarily chosen to represent concepts. Once selected, however, signs lose their arbitrary and contingent character and become fixed. Language is part of the "collective mind of the community of speakers" (Saussere 1966: 96). Because members know the rules of their system and its signs, they can use it to exchange information. Communication is always built upon previously determined signs; it makes sense only insofar as it conforms to patterns of communication that made sense in the past (Luhmann 1985; 1997). Similarly, ritual acts adhere to a previously determined structure—rituals are "rule-bound acts" and are never improvised (Deutsch 1991: 16–17).

Whatever their personal motivations and subjective thoughts, participants in a ritual can only coordinate their actions by conforming to the established structure of ritual. New forms of socially meaningful action can only be created when members manipulate previously existing forms.

Rules, Rituals, and Collective Identity

Human beings are born in a state of openness—"world-openness" (Gehlen 1956; Plessner 1964). Precisely because we are naturally free of instinctual directives (*instinktarm*), we are able to adapt to countless forms of social life. Social rules and customs are to humans as instincts are to animals. Without internal instincts to guide them, people survive in the world by accepting the way of life and patterns of behavior established by their predecessors:

> All that we may be sure of so far is that residual instincts provide no guarantee of any kind for lasting forms of behavior. Instinctively, nothing requires that man act regularly and in the same manner on the same occasions. There are no natural or social (and certainly not relative to the external environment) drives or instincts that could as biological factors assure behavioral stability. Because of this world-openness and separation from instincts, nothing guarantees that any kind of social action can arise, and if it does arise, that it will not fall apart tomorrow. Institutions fill exactly this gap—they stand in the place of the inherent attachments that are missing between humans. (Gehlen 1956: 178)

The most elementary kind of social institution, rituals make normal social interaction possible. Unified through a common identity, individuals are able to coordinate their efforts toward instrumental ends.

The regulations of the Weaverland community protect the integrity of the group by imposing a clearly defined life-style upon all members. Regardless of what he believes in his heart, a "true" Mennonite conforms to the prescriptions of his church and identifies with its symbols.

Ritual symbols and meanings are too indeterminate and
their schemes too flexible to lend themselves to any
simple process of instilling fixed ideas. Indeed, in terms
of its scope, dependence, and legitimation, the type of
authority formulated by ritualization tends to make ritual activities effective in grounding and displaying a
sense of community *without* overriding the autonomy
of individuals or subgroups. (Bell 1992: 221–22)

The ritual practices and symbols of the Weaverland Church
consolidate individuals while allowing each member to freely inter-
pret the spiritual significance of his actions. There is external con-
straint in ritual practice, but there is also freedom in interpretation.

The Conference Rules function to hide the diversity that
would otherwise separate individuals. When members dress alike,
drive the same cars, and have the same jobs, it becomes easier for
them to believe in their common identity.

When members see themselves cooperating to perform mech-
anized, rule-governed rituals, they gain confidence in their ability
to coordinate collective action in real life. The predictable, rou-
tinized actions performed in the safety of the church serve as desir-
able models for all other actions during the week. Ritual is a peti-
tion: let us be as unified outside this ritual as we have been inside
it. Religious interaction serves as a foundation for all other interaction. It brings individuals together in time and space, providing
a stage, scenery, script, and props. After worshipping together, the
actors leave the church prepared to live and work as members of a
visible community.

Weaverland Mennonites in New York State demonstrate that
it is possible for the members of a social group to coordinate very
precise collective activity without sharing the same motivation or
subjective meaning. Orthopraxis does not require orthodoxis. I
have described the uniform manner in which Weaverland Mennonites conform to established social facts and follow procedural

rules of ritual, but I have also shown that, when called upon to give accounts, they explain the "meaning" of their behavior in different ways. Members of the group have not taken an interest in uncovering and repairing this apparent disjuncture. Members honestly and openly profess that their peers believe as they do. As Gehlen concluded (1956: 29), "forms are the food of faith." They know one another by their works. Whatever their individual religious beliefs happen to be, Old Order Mennonites are socially integrated because they adhere to the same behavioral forms.

Emile Durkheim (1965: 463–64) maintained that people who truly lead the religious life and have a direct sensation of what it really is, understand that, "the real function of religion is not to make us think, to enrich our knowledge, nor to add to the conceptions which we owe to science others of another origin and another character, but rather, it is to make us act, to aid us to live."

Several years ago, when my neighbor's cow went dry and I went down the road to get milk from strangers, I encountered a group of people who know how to live.

Note

1. *A Collection of Psalms and Hymns* 1977: 228.

References

Bell, Catherine. 1992. *Ritual Theory, Ritual Practice*. New York: Oxford University Press.

Benowitz, Jean-Paul. 1996. "The Mennonites of Pennsylvania: A House Divided." *Pennsylvania Folklife* 46 (1):2–19.

Berger, Peter. 1990. *The Sacred Canopy*. NY: Doubleday.

Berger, Peter and Thomas Luckmann. 1966. *The Social Construction of Reality*. Garden City, New York: Doubleday.

Blake, Judith and Kingsley Davis. 1964. "Norms, Values, and Sanctions." Pp. 456–84 in *Handbook of Modern Sociology*. Edited by Robert E. L. Faris. Chicago: Rand McNally.

Cohen, A.P. 1985. *The Symbolic Construction of Community*. New York: Tavistock.

A Collection of Psalms and Hymns. 1977. Compiled by a Committee of Mennonites. Philadelphia: National Publishing Co.

Confession of Faith of the Mennonites. 1996. Published by the Weaverland Conference.

Confession of Faith of the Mennonites. 1989. Published by the Committee, Old Order Mennonites.

Crocker, Christopher. 1973. "Ritual and the Development of Social Structure: Liminality and Inversion." Pp. 47–86 in *The Roots of Ritual*. Edited by James D. Shaughnessy. Grand Rapids, MI: William B. Eerdmans.

Dahm, Karl Wilhelm, Niklas Luhmann, and Dieter Stoodt. 1972. *Religion: System und Sozialisation*. Darmstadt: Luchterhand.

Dallas Morning News. 1995. "Mennonites Fall Prey to Profits of Drugs" (July 2): A26.

Deutsch, Eliot. 1991. "Community as Ritual Participation." Pp. 15–25 in *On Community*. Edited by Leroy S. Rouner. Notre Dame, IN: University of Notre Dame Press.

Durkheim, Emile. 1953. *Sociology and Philosophy*. Glencoe, IL: Free Press.

_____.1964. *The Division of Labor in Society*. New York: Free Press.

_____. 1965. *The Elementary Forms of the Religious Life*. New York: Free Press.

Dyck, Cornelius. 1981. *An Introduction to Mennonite History: A Popular History of the Anabaptists and Mennonites*. Scotsdale, PA: Herald Press.

Erikson, Kai T. 1966. *Wayward Puritians*. New York: John Wiley.

Family Life. 1983. 12:3.

Family Life. 1984a. 2:3.

Family Life. 1984b. 7:4.

Family Life. 1984c. 10:13–14.

Family Life. 1993. 7:2,19.

Fretz, J. Winfield. 1989. *The Waterloo Mennonites: A Community in Paradox*. Waterloo, Ontario: Wilfrid Laurier University Press.

Gehlen, Arnold. 1956. *Urmensch und Spaetkultur*. Bonn: Athenaeum.

Gilbert, Margaret. 1989. *On Social Facts*. New York: Routledge.

Gluckman, Max. 1954. *Rituals of Rebellion in South-East Africa*. Manchester: Manchester University Press.

_____. 1962. "Les Rites de Passage." Pp. 1–52 in *Essays on the Ritual of Social Relations*. Edited by Max Gluckman and C.D. Forde. Manchester: Manchester University Press.

Graber, Robert B. 1984. "An Amiable Mennonite Schism: The Origin of the Eastern Pennsylvania Mennonite Church." *Pennsylvania Mennonite Heritage* 7 (October):2–10.

Harrison, Jane Ellen. 1912. *Themis: A Study of the Social Origins of Greek Religion*. Cambridge: Cambridge University Press.

Herald American. 1994. "New York Farmers" (September 11):14.

Home Messenger. 1977. "On That Farm Near Martindale" 14 (May):5.

Home Messenger. 1994. "The Christian Woman's Veiling" 31 (June):6.

Hoover, Amos B. 1982. *The Jonas Martin Era*. Denver, PA: Author.

Hostetler, John A. 1993. *Amish Society*. Baltimore: Johns Hopkins University Press.

Kephart, William M. and William W. Zellner. 1994. *Extraordinary Groups*. New York: St. Martin's Press.

Kluckhohn, Clyde. 1949. *Mirror for Man*. New York: Whittlesey House.

Kniss, Fred. 1996. "Ideas and Symbols as Resources in Intrareligious Conflict: The Case of American Mennonites." *Sociology of Religion* 57 (Spring):7–23.

Loewen, Howard John. 1985. *One Lord, One Church, One Hope and One God: Mennonite Confessions of Faith*. Elkhart, IN: Institute of Mennonite Studies.

Los Angeles Times. 1998. "With Drug Arrests, Urban Grit Smudges Amish Life" (June 25):A1.

Luhmann, Niklas. 1981. "The Improbability of Communication." *International Social Science Journal* 33:122–32.

———. 1985. "Society, Meaning, Religion-Based on Self-Reference." *Sociological Analysis* 46:5–20.

———. 1991. "Religion and Society." *Sociologia Internationalis* 29:133–39.

———. 1994. "'What Is the Case?' and 'What Lies Behind It?' The Two Sociologies and the Theory of Society." *Sociological Theory* 12:126–39.

———. 1997. *Die Gesellschaft der Gesellschaft*. Frankfurt am Main: Suhrkamp.

Lyman, Stanford M. and Marvin B. Scott. 1989. *A Sociology of the Absurd*. Dix Hills, NY: General Hall.

Mannheim, Karl. 1982. "Ideologische und soziologische Interpretation der geistigen Gebilde." Pp. 213–30 in *Der Streit um die Wissenssoziologie*. Edited by Volker Meja and Nico Stehr. Frankfurt: Suhrkamp.

Martin, David L. 1986. *Handbook for Creative Teaching*. Crockett, KY: Rod and Staff.

Martin, Raymond S. and Elizabeth S. Martin. 1985. *Bishop Jonas H. Martin, His Life and Genealogy*. Baltimore: Gateway Press, Inc.

Mennonite Calender of Weaverland Conference. 2000. Ephrata, PA: Grace Press.

The Mennonite Encyclopedia. 1959. Scottdale, PA: Mennonite Publishing House.

Merton, Robert K. 1968. *Social Theory and Social Structure*. New York: Free Press.

Mizruchi, Ephraim H. and Robert Perrucci. 1973. "Norm Qualities and Deviant Behavior." Pp. 304–14 in *The Substance of Sociology*. Edited by Ephraim H. Mizruchi. New York: Meredith.

Not To Be Modern. 1988. Directed by Victoria Larimore. Maui, HI: Media Plus Inc.

Oxford English Dictionary. 1971. Oxford: Oxford University Press.

Parsons, Talcott and Edward A. Shils. 1951. *Toward a General Theory of Action*. New York: Harper and Row.

Plessner, Helmut. 1964. *Conditio humana*. Pfullingen: Guenther Neske.

Post Standard. 1996. "Mennonites Unite After Tragedy" (September 3):1.

Redekop, Calvin Wall. 1969. *The Old Colony Mennonites*. Baltimore: Johns Hopkins University Press.

Redekop, Calvin, Stephen C. Ainlay, and Robert Siemens. 1995. *Mennonite Entreprenuers*. Baltimore: Johns Hopkins.

Redfield, Robert. 1947. "The Folk Society." *American Journal of Sociology* 52:293–308.

Sanderson, Stephen K. 1991. *Macrosociology*. New York: HarperCollins.

Saussere, Ferdinand de. 1966. *Course in General Linguistics*. New York: McGraw-Hill.

Schlabach, Theron F. 1985. *Peace, Faith, Nation*. Scottdale, PA: Herald Press.

Schutz, Alfred. 1967. *The Phenomenology of the Social World*. Evanston, IL: Northwestern University Press.

Scott, Marvin B. and Stanford M. Lyman. 1973. "Accounts." Pp. 326–50 in *The Substance of Sociology*. Edited by Ephraim H. Mizruchi. New York: Meredith.

Scott, Stephen. 1996. *Old Order and Conservative Mennonite Groups*. Intercourse, PA: Good Books.

Simmel, Georg. 1950. *The Sociology of George Simmel*. Glencoe, IL: Free Press.

Thompson, Kenneth. 1986. *Beliefs and Ideology*. New York: Tavistock.

Toennies, Ferdinand. 1963. *Community and Society*. New York: Harper and Row.

USDA. 1997. *Census of Agriculture—State Data: Pennsylvania and New York*. Washington DC: National Agricultural Statistics Service.

———. 1999. *Departmental Regulation: 9700*. Washington DC: U.S. Department of Agriculture.

Vidich, Arthur J. and Standford M. Lyman. 1994. "Qualitative Methods: Their History in Sociology and Anthropology." Pp. 23–59 in *Handbook of Qualitative Research*. Edited by Norman K. Denzin and Yvonna S. Lincoln. Thousand Oaks, CA: Sage.

Wallwork, Ernest. 1972. *Durkheim: Morality and Milieu*. Cambridge, MA: Harvard University Press.

———. 1985. "Durkheim's Early Sociology of Religion." *Sociological Analysis* 46 (3): 201–18.

Weber, Max. 1972. *Wirtschaft und Gesellschaft*. Tuebingen: J.C.B. Mohr.

———. 1988. *Gesammelte Aufsaetze zur Religionssoziologie*. Tuebingen: J.C.B. Mohr.

Weiler, Lloyd M. 1995. "A Historical Overview of Weaverland Conference Origins." Appendix in *Directory of the Members and Their Families Who Attend the Weaverland Conference Mennonite Churches Located in Pennsylvania, Virginia, Missouri, New York, and Wisconsin*. Compiled by Ruth Ann Wise and Lucille Martin. Womelsdorf, PA: The Compilers.

Wenger, Eli D. 1989. *The Weaverland Mennonites*. New Holland, PA: Lewis B. Groff.

Wenger, J.C. 1966. *The Mennonite Church in America*. Scottdale, PA: Herald Press.

Winch, Peter. 1977. *The Idea of a Social Science and Its Relation to Philosophy*. Atlantic Highlands, NJ: Humanities Press.

Wise, Ruth Ann and Lucille Martin. 1990; 1995. *Directory of the Members and Their Families Who Attend the Weaverland Conference Mennonite Churches Located in Pennsylvania, Virginia, Missouri, and New York, and Wisconsin*. Compiled by Ruth Ann Wise and Lucile Martin. Womelsdorg, PA: The Compilers.

Yetman, Norman R. 1991. *Majority and Minority*. Boston: Allyn and Bacon.

Zito, G.V. 1983. "A Sociology of Heresy." *Sociological Analysis* 44:123–30.

Index

165